THEATRE SYMPOSIUM
A PUBLICATION OF THE SOUTHEASTERN THEATRE CONFERENCE

The Prop's the Thing: Stage Properties Reconsidered

Volume 18

Published by the

Southeastern Theatre Conference and

The University of Alabama Press

THEATRE SYMPOSIUM is published annually by the Southeastern Theatre Conference, Inc. (SETC), and by The University of Alabama Press. SETC nonstudent members receive the journal as a part of their membership under rules determined by SETC. For information on membership write to SETC, P.O. Box 9868, Greensboro, NC 27429-0868. All other inquiries regarding subscriptions, circulation, purchase of individual copies, and requests to reprint materials should be addressed to The University of Alabama Press, Box 870380, Tuscaloosa, AL 35487-0380.

THEATRE SYMPOSIUM publishes works of scholarship resulting from a single-topic meeting held on a southeastern university campus each spring. A call for papers to be presented at that meeting is widely publicized each autumn for the following spring. Information about the next symposium is available from the editor, J. K. Curry, Department of Theatre and Dance, P.O. Box 7264, Wake Forest University, Winston-Salem, NC, 27109, curryjk@wfu.edu.

THEATRE SYMPOSIUM
A PUBLICATION OF THE SOUTHEASTERN THEATRE CONFERENCE

Volume 18 2010

Contents

Introduction

HUMBLE STAGE properties are objects that often escape notice when they are functioning properly. Though insignificant at first glance, theatrical props are worthy of our attention, and not only because of the potential of the inappropriate or malfunctioning prop to destroy illusion and disrupt a performance. It is equally fascinating to consider how props can be skillfully employed by playwrights and other theatre artists. An invitation to theatre scholars and practitioners to take a fresh look at props, "The Prop's the Thing: Stage Properties Reconsidered" was selected as the theme of the 2009 SETC Theatre Symposium held at Wake Forest University in Winston-Salem, North Carolina.

Anchoring the event were keynote presentations by two experts who, from very different perspectives, each provided unique knowledge and insights, practical and theoretical, about how props work in the theatre. Bland M. Wade Jr., director of the Stage Properties Program at the University of North Carolina School of the Arts, offered a first-person perspective on the typical challenges of creating stage props in his talk, "Through the Eyes of the Property Director." Wade also led symposium attendees on an informative guided tour of the impressive Scenic and Property Studios at the UNC School of the Arts. The other keynote speaker, Andrew Sofer, has made a significant contribution to the academic study of props with his book *The Stage Life of Props* (2003). Indeed, his work was widely cited by other presenters. In his paper, "'Take up the Bodies': Shakespeare's Body Parts, Babies, and Corpses," Sofer reconsidered his earlier position on "whether the human body could become a prop" and reviewed a variety of methods for disposing of corpses on the Shakespearean stage. Following Sofer's presentation, symposium participants had a chance to view the Wake Forest University Theatre production of *King Lear,* which included a full range of "corpse as prop" removal methods.

The other essays included in this collection approach the subject of stage properties from several angles, including close examination of the use of props by individual playwrights in many different periods of theatre history. In "'Summon up the Blood': The Stylized (or Sticky) Stuff of Violence in Three Plays by Sarah Kane," Christine Woodworth addresses the practical challenges presented by blood used as a stage prop, while identifying three different strategies employed by playwright Sarah Kane in presenting violence and blood onstage. Sarah Powers examines prop use in classical Greece in "Helen's Theatrical *Mêchanê:* Props and Costumes in Euripides' *Helen,*" focusing on abundant prop use as a marker of comedy. Euripides' experimentation with props, parodied by Aristophanes, is a key element in his challenge of genre conventions.

In "A Cannonade of Weapons: Signs of Transgression in the Early *Commedia dell'arte,*" Kyna Hamill looks at the use of prop weapons to mark social status as well as the transgression of prescribed social roles. When lower-class characters wield weapons inappropriately or overload themselves with too many, the props are used to great comic effect. Christopher J. Mitchell demonstrates that judicious use of props was a central element of the dramaturgy of August Strindberg's chamber plays in "Adding Some 'PEP' ('Proto-Expressionistic Props') to the Swedish Stage: Strindberg's Property Usage and His Intima Teater." The symbolic objects reveal the characters' private anguish and tormented pasts.

Sometimes a single key property is crucial to the construction of the dramatic action. In "Rattle Away at Your Bin: Women, Community, and Bin Lids in Northern Irish Drama," Eleanor Owicki explores the theatrical power of an ordinary object that has been invested with cultural significance. In this case it is a rubbish bin lid, whose culturally specific meaning is used and also subverted in the Charabanc company's play *Somewhere over the Balcony.* Adrienne C. Macki traces the stage evolution of a single strikingly significant prop in "Bearing Witness: The Noose as an Iconic Prop in African American Theatre." Macki identifies three separate phases of lynching drama, distinguished by the presence or absence of the noose and the manner in which the evocative prop is utilized. Stefani Overman-Tsai examines another object of cultural significance in "Hawaiian Culture Propped High with Meaning: The Lei Hoaka in Victoria Nalani Kneubuhl's *Emmalehua.*" She demonstrates that through their interaction with a specific stage prop, the lei hoaka, characters in this play reveal their postcolonial struggle to balance traditional cultural practices against the pressure of Americanization.

The next two essays offer a broader exploration of how stage props are perceived and comprehended by audiences. In his article "Revisiting Eva Marie Saint's White Glove: On Props, Neurons, Subtext, and Empathy," Andrew Kimbrough moves from an examination of actors' use of props to a consideration of audience response to performance. From the perspective of cognitive studies, empathic audience response to an actor manipulating a stage prop is connected to the audience's experience relating to objects in everyday life. In another essay informed by cognitive studies, "From Props to Affordances: An Ecological Approach to Theatrical Objects," Teemu Paavolainen suggests a way to raise the status of props within theatre research. Employing an ecological perspective, he draws attention to the idea that audience members viewing any theatre production will perceive the potential actions various props afford.

One of the usual pleasures of *Theatre Symposium* is that it invites a range of theatre specialists to share their expertise and engage in lively conversation about a topic of mutual interest. In addition to the theatre practitioner and the theatre scholar invited to present keynote addresses, the other presenters and attendees at this year's symposium included a mix of prop directors and prop masters, theatre historians and theorists. Many also had experience as directors, performers, or designers, and years of theatre-going to draw on while exchanging insights about theatrical props. I would like to thank all the participants in the 2009 symposium. In addition to the scholars whose work is included in this volume, presenters included Noreen C. Barnes, Hope Bernard, Rachel Linn Bonds, Lindy M. Bumgarner, Steve Earnest, Stephen Harrick, Eric Hart, Stewart Hawley, Joy Shihyi Huang, Casey Kaleba, Milton Loayza, Sarah Grace Marsh, Wes D. Pearce, Zackary Ross, and Angela Sweigart-Gallagher.

The 2009 symposium event was supported by the Wake Forest Department of Theatre and Dance and the Wake Forest University Theatre's Babcock Fund. I would like to thank my Wake Forest colleagues who provided encouragement and assistance, including shuttling symposium goers to and from the airport. For guidance in organizing and preparing both the symposium event and this volume, I would like to thank the previous editors of *Theatre Symposium*, especially founding editor Phil Hill and *Theatre Symposium* Steering Committee chair Scott Phillips. Thanks also to my immediate predecessor, Jay Malarcher; associate editor E. Bert Wallace; SETC executive director Betsey Baun; and Dan Waterman at The University of Alabama Press.

J. K. Curry
Wake Forest University

Through the Eyes of the Property Director

Bland M. Wade Jr.

The following remarks are excerpts from his Theatre Symposium address.

LET US START at the very beginning with defining a prop. If you were to go into your living room at home and take out everything except the bare walls, ceiling, and floor, you would have left what we call scenery. All of the other things in the room would be props, including the ceiling fixtures, rugs on the floor, and trash in the trash can. You may ask yourself, "Who would want a job working with props?" My friends and family ask me what it is that I do. When I reply that I am a property director, they immediately think I manage real estate. It can be very confusing to those not in the world of theatre. I have found that using what I call the "house analogy" puts it in terms they understand.

The *director* is the homeowner (also the client, the one with ideas); it is the director's family (the actors) that will live in this space. The *designer* is the architect and interior designer. The *technical director* is the engineer and contractor, the one who actually builds the house. The *property director* is the interior decorator, the plumber, the cabinetmaker, the upholsterer, the gardener, the handyman. He or she cooks your meals, washes your dishes, takes care of your pets, and so on.

There is not much difference in props for theatre, television, and film. A coffee cup onstage is a coffee cup on television, is a coffee cup on the big screen. There are definitely different responsibilities and different vocabulary, but a good property artisan can move in and out of these different worlds fairly easily.

I use the term *property director* as opposed to *property master*. There is a movement in the industry to change the name from property master to property director, because the latter term more adequately describes what the position has become. Historically the property master was a part of the scenery crew, who had mastered the various crafts and finished carpentry. His or her job was to procure, repair, and build the props needed for a particular production. The technical director oversaw the budget needs, staffing, and work schedule. Today, property directors usually have their own shop, where they manage their own budgets, staffing, and work schedules. This is in no way implying that the term *property master* does not exist: it still does, both out of tradition and out of the established structure of organizations.

As a prop person, you have to read between the lines. If a stage direction reads, "Bob enters stage left with a cigarette," what does that mean to props? A simple stage direction could lead to a half page of props and a plethora of questions. Is the cigarette lit? Does the facility allow smoking? Does the actor smoke? What kind of cigarette? Is it in a soft pack, hard pack, or cigarette case, or is it a single smoke? How is it lit? How does the actor dispose of it? What are the materials of the costumes? Are they flammable? Asking as many questions up front will eliminate many additions to the prop list during the rehearsal process.

I like to keep in mind what I call the "property triangle," which consists of three points: quality, fast, and cheap. I refer to this quite a bit with both designers and directors. You may pick two points and only two. You may choose quality and fast, but it will not be cheap. Or, cheap and fast, but it will lack quality. Or, quality and cheap, will not be fast.

Property artisans approach properties like sculpture. More often than not, you are attempting to re-create something from found objects. Many times one can be overwhelmed by the size and complexity of a piece and not know where to start. First, look at the individual shapes and what they remind you of. Focus on solving one problem at a time, and by the end you will have a completed piece. However, one must never be afraid to scrap an idea and start over. Too many spend countless hours and resources on a process that is riddled with problems and doomed to fail. Keep it simple, and remember that in the prop world if it can go wrong, it will. Set decorating is basically the same; we look at a set as a still life.

Sometimes an artisan is re-creating something that exists or existed, other times creating things that do not exist, be it futuristic or fantasy. When looking at futuristic properties, the artisan will research the evolution of the object over the past century and, based on that knowledge, predict its evolution into the future. Over my career I have found futuristic props along with fantasy props, such as a glowing orb on a staff, to be the most interesting. But remember: for every fantasy prop there is a coffee cup.[1]

Property directors are problem solvers, troubleshooters, inventors, and jacks-of-all-trades. The more skills you have, the more employable you are. We are historians as well. Accuracy is very important. There will always be someone in the audience who will know the difference, and cannot wait to call you on it. Also, just because you found something in research does not make it the best choice. The audience has to believe it. Right or wrong, the audience will have a preconceived idea of what a particular period or prop should look like. While some say that the stage and its performers are there to educate the audience—and I do not disagree with this—do not keep the focus entirely on the education of the audience. If you do, the play will lose its entertainment value. A well-propped show usually goes unnoticed.

How is the property artisan essential to theatre? You can always cut scenery or use a bare stage with actors in street clothes under work lights, but the need for props will still be there. Companies will try and save money by cutting the need for scenery, only to find that they spend the same amount with the director and designer trying to fill the space with props. Props are the catalyst for laughter and tears. Slapstick comedy would not be very funny without its rubber hammer or nightstick. And how many tears are shed when Romeo drinks from the poison vial? Props fill an important role and can destroy a scene or the entire production. In *West Side Story,* if the gun does not fire, we have no ending; Tony has to die. In *Wait until Dark,* if the refrigerator light does not work, the scene is destroyed.

The property director should always have a backup plan or two. A production of *West Side Story* that I worked had the assistant stage manager backstage with a gun in the event the gun misfired onstage. However, without the assistant stage manager having quick reflexes, this could become comical and destroy the emotional ending of the production. As a third layer, I gave the actor a switchblade to carry in his back pocket in the event of gun mishaps. All of these scenarios were planned out and rehearsed; by doing so, we had a flawless run.

Remember that the health and safety of the actors are in the hands of the property artisan. You do not want to give the cast food poisoning from your lack of cleanliness or poor food preparation. The most dangerous area is weapons; whether swords, guns, or sticks, any use of weapons must be staged, rehearsed, and planned. Also, remember if the prop you hand to an actor looks like garbage, he will treat it like garbage. In the end, a production without actors is nothing but a window display.

Note

1. An excellent, free resource for any new or established property artisan can be found at www.prophandbook.com. This site was written by Sandra Strawn at the University of Wisconsin–Milwaukee.

"Summon up the Blood"

The Stylized (or Sticky) Stuff of Violence in Three Plays by Sarah Kane

Christine Woodworth

If we are what people say we are, let us take our delight in the blood of men.

So said Tertullian in his love letter to the theatre, *On the Spectacles*.[1] Tertullian, it seems, was not far off, as our theatrical histories are awash with blood—real and imagined. Among the complex rituals associated with the ancient Athenian City Dionysia, a blood sacrifice served as a sacred offering to the gods.[2] The blood sports of Imperial Rome went so far as to fatten up gladiatorial combatants in order to slow the flow of their blood upon injury so that spectators had longer to revel in their agony.[3] Medieval theatre, particularly in the performances of the Cycle plays, dripped with a blood whose symbolic resonances were complexly layered and remain hotly contested. Elizabethan plays were riddled with stabbings, decapitations, and disembowelments, calling for props as simple as "sponges of vinegar" and as complex as bladders filled with sheep's blood and entrails.[4] France's late nineteenth- and early twentieth-century Grand-Guignol theatre has been characterized as a theatre of excess in terms of its horrific representations. Their productions were so gory, in fact, that according to legend, the theatre had to employ a doctor to revive theatre patrons that fainted at the sight of the tortures and violence.[5]

The use of blood onstage is fraught with religious, social, and practical concerns. The roots of Western and non-Western theatre are soaked in the blood of ceremonial sacrifice. For centuries on the stage, blood has vexed those responsible for its manufacture and execution. When used as a prop, blood marks the level of abstraction of a particular piece of theatre. Blood may be realistic, as in the sheep's blood bladders of the Renaissance, or over the top, as in the gruesome offerings of the Grand-Guignol, or stylized, as with the dyed red cotton cloths of Kabuki. The all-too-brief canon of Sarah Kane, notorious "bad girl" of the British stage, offers three distinct treatments of blood that exemplify these three demarcations: realistic, excessive, and stylized. *Blasted, Phaedra's Love,* and *Cleansed* serve as productive points of departure for the development of a "grammar of blood" as well as a literary and performative genealogy of blood on the stage. As Andrew Sofer asserts, "The stage life of props extends beyond their journey within a given play. . . . As they move from play to play and from period to period, objects accrue intertextual resonance as they absorb and embody the theatrical past."[6] While often falling within the domain of makeup, stage blood can also be situated within several categories of props, as explicated by Sofer. Blood that is manipulated by an actor rather than merely worn can take on a number of the "lives" of stage props that Sofer sets forth.[7] This examination of three of Kane's plays will address the practical considerations involved in the use of stage blood, the ways in which blood operates referentially, and the perils of blood as a potentially "recalcitrant prop."[8] While the use of blood in *Blasted, Phaedra's Love,* and *Cleansed* does not necessarily break new ground for prop artisans, Kane's works offer contemporary examples of the continuously vexing and perpetually haunted use of blood as a stage prop.

Kane's first play, *Blasted,* premiered in 1995 and caused a firestorm among critics. Featuring three characters—the jaded journalist, Ian, the developmentally challenged Cate, and the desperate Soldier—the entirety of the action takes place in a hotel room in Leeds. The frightening dynamic between Cate and Ian escalates to rape, which occurs in the time lapse between the first two scenes. At the end of scene 2, the seemingly distant war intrudes itself upon Cate and Ian's protective space as the Soldier forces his way into the room and additional horrors ensue. Over the course of *Blasted,* blood is called for in a number of ways. Ian's eyes are sucked out and eaten by the Soldier; the Soldier has "blown his own brains out" between scenes 3 and 4, which requires blood spatter and brain tissue; Ian eats the dead baby that Cate has buried in the hotel room floor; and, at the end of the play, Cate enters with "blood seeping from between her legs" having traded her body for food.[9] Incidents such as these greatly upset the critics in 1995.[10] More recently, however, *Blasted* made its New York debut at Soho Rep in the fall of 2008. The production garnered surprising accolades, landing on many critics' Best of 2008 lists.

Although *Blasted* veers away from realism formally, the use of blood in the Soho Rep production was highly realistic. Realistic stagings of blood present countless challenges to prop designers, from research to experimentation to integration into the rehearsal process to cleanup.

Makeup and special effects artist (and University of North Carolina School of the Arts faculty member) Michael Meyer has described his line of work as a "bloody industry" and has spoken about the rather graphic nature of research for prop and makeup design that involves blood, injury, and death.[11] Although the makeup design, scars, and such were the responsibility of the costume and wardrobe staff, Sarah Birdhouse, the prop designer for the Soho Rep production, had to address several fairly explicit uses of blood. She related that "I had to deal with the dead baby, which was a distressing challenge. I literally Google imaged 'dead baby,' and there were numerous images to use."[12] Alexis Soloski, writing for the *Village Voice*, noted that "The prop designer, Sarah Birdhouse, has her hands full—and rather sticky—designing that edible baby filled with stage blood."[13] Birdhouse clarified that there was much more than stage blood in the hollowed-out doll used in the production. She described the ingredients that she experimented with: "I did lots of samples of possible guts, using edible stage blood, Jell-O, figs, dates, and tortillas. I also used rice paper to seal the guts pack I made. It was basically a trial and error job, as is most blood work." In what can only be characterized as an unusual taste test, actor Reed Birney, who played Ian, was given the various samples to try in order to "work out a ratio of how much blood to Jell-O, etc., was required." Hundreds of varieties of stage blood are available commercially. Most designers, however, craft their own much the way Birdhouse described, through the process of trial and error. Meyer has estimated that there are at least five thousand different recipes for stage blood. Birdhouse's favorite commercial blood is Nick Dudman's, which, when budgets allow, she prefers to use instead of making blood from scratch. When a given recipe or formula is not perfect, the blood runs the risk of becoming what Sofer describes as a recalcitrant prop, not properly functioning in the manner it was intended.

Edible blood in particular presents all sorts of challenges in terms of safety, palatability, preparation, and disposal. Blood devised from foodstuffs cannot exist out of time because of concerns regarding ingredients congealing or going bad. Time is also a concern for stage blood that gets applied to more sensitive regions of an actor's body. Birdhouse shared that the eye blood, which often has a very short life, was integrated into the rehearsal process fairly early and involved a collaboration between the actors, costume designer, and fight choreographer. For the blood following the Soldier's suicide, Birdhouse again found herself turning to some edible ingredients. This particular use of blood brought yet another set of challenges in that it needed to be cleaned up completely every night. Birdhouse stated that "for the blood and brains splatter I made some washable blood (the basic formula: Karo syrup, food coloring, Hershey's chocolate syrup, and washing detergent) and added some frozen cherries as texture. It is always a risk using food coloring as it doesn't wash out well from pale carpets, but *Blasted* had a terrible budget so I couldn't afford washable blood."[14]

Soho Rep currently resides in a fairly intimate performance space, which, as Birdhouse confessed, "made the show even more horrifying." The production of *Blasted* brought new resonance to Aleks Sierz's designation of Kane's writing as "In-Yer-Face."[15] Such proximity also created several challenges in regards to the use of blood. In an interview with Patrick Healy of the *New York Times*, actor Marin Ireland, who played Cate, described the opening of scene 2, following Ian's rape of Cate: "For a little while we were planning to have blood all over my leg, but that went away for purely logistical reasons, because I'd have to have it on [at] the top of the show. . . . We couldn't find any blood that wouldn't stick to my pants."[16]

The blood called for in *Blasted* clearly presents numerous practical challenges. On another level, however, the blood (and the violence that causes it) situates *Blasted* in a larger historical context. In his *New York Times* article, Mark Blankenship describes the intrusion of the war into the hotel room as a "Jacobean style of horror."[17] "Neo-Jacobeanism" has been used, especially by Graham Saunders, in describing the work of Kane. Highlighting what Mark Ravenhill calls her "classical sensibility,"[18] Saunders states that, "like the Jacobean drama of William Shakespeare, Thomas Middleton and John Webster, Kane manages to condense great themes such as war and human salvation down to a series of stark memorable theatrical images." Saunders traces the legacy of Jacobean playwrights through the shocking playwrights of the 1960s and 1970s (Bond, Barker, etc.) who were also influential for Kane.[19] In Kane's first interview following the debut of *Blasted*, she spoke with David Benedict of the *Independent* about her use of violence in the play: "There is, she says, 'no real debate in this country [England] about how you represent violence in art. We don't know how to talk about it, we don't know how to deal with it. The violence in this play is completely de-glamorised. It's just presented. . . . I wrote it to tell the truth. Of course that's shocking. Take the glamour out of violence and it becomes utterly repulsive. Would people seriously prefer it if the violence was appealing?' "[20]

Phaedra's Love, Kane's second play, which premiered at London's Gate Theatre in 1996 and which Kate Bassett referred to as an "extravaganza of grisliness," ended with an almost literal bloodbath for the audience.[21] *Phaedra's Love* can be situated with other over-the-top, excessively bloody pieces such as Martin McDonagh's *The Lieutenant of Inishmore* and George Reinblatt, Frank Cipolla, Melissa Morris, and Christopher Bond's campy

Evil Dead the Musical. The Toronto production of *Evil Dead* ran for almost four hundred performances and, as *Toronto Star* theatre critic Richard Ouzounian stated, "Gore spurts from the walls, from the ceiling, from every chopped-up demon and it sprays with mad abandon into the audience. If you're not in the designated 'Splatter Zone,' you're supposedly safe, but hey, what's the point of safety at a show like this?"[22] Stage blood in extremis presents even more challenges to all involved in production due to the sheer volume of blood required. A recent production of *The Lieutenant of Inishmore* at Signature Theatre in Arlington, Virginia, required a weekly fumigation of the theatre due to the infestation of fruit flies, drawn to the chocolate-based blood.[23] While *Phaedra's Love, The Lieutenant of Inishmore,* and *Evil Dead the Musical* are radically different in terms of genre, tone, and style, they are united by the gallons of blood they require.

Kane, dissatisfied with some of the images in the Royal Court production of *Blasted,* decided to direct *Phaedra's Love* herself. The Gate Theatre invited Kane to write *Phaedra's Love* as part of their "New Plays, Ancient Sources" season.[24] *Phaedra's Love* is an adaptation of Seneca's *Phaedra.* Gone are the civilizing, neoclassic concerns of Racine's retelling of the tale. Instead, Kane foregrounds the baseness of humanity, which she views as having spiraled into dehumanized extremes in the face of capitalist waste. Ken Urban described the original production of *Phaedra's Love* as a "mess of stage blood and fake intestines."[25] The violence and use of blood were so extreme that audience members allegedly vomited at the premiere. Renaissance Austin Theatre Company produced *Phaedra's Love* in 2005 in a production that, according to one reviewer, "includes incest, murder, rape, and graphic scenes that require splash guards."[26] The Loose Canon theatre company in Dublin staged a production in 2008 and utilized so much blood that the "ensemble unroll[ed] plastic sheeting across the stage to deal with the blood flow."[27]

In the final scene of the play, an angry mob has convened outside the court, waiting for Hippolytus to emerge. Theseus has returned, having mourned over Phaedra's funeral pyre in the previous scene. He has disguised himself in order to rile up the mob so that Hippolytus can be killed. Strophe has also disguised herself in order to defend Hippolytus. Although this final scene is just as brief as those that came before, it is rich with commentary on contemporary society. It is also incredibly violent. As Charles Spencer of the *Daily Telegraph* wrote, "By now we are 50 minutes into the hour-long play, and by Kane's standards, very little has happened. She makes up for it in the last 10." In this final scene Hippolytus breaks free of the police escort and throws himself into the crowd where he recognizes his father. The mob quickly starts to attack and torture him. As Strophe attempts to defend him, Theseus rapes her and then slits her throat. In the midst of all of this, members of the audience rise up and join the fray. As Michael Coveney of the *Observer* noted, "actors among the squatting audience rise like a lynch mob to take matters into their own violent hands, a powerful, genuinely effective equivalent of the monster rising from the angry sea to frighten the prince's horses."[28] As many of the critics pointed out, Hippolytus's torture and death were accompanied by the removal of body parts that were then thrown—dripping—over the heads of the audience. Notably, Hippolytus's genitals are cut off, thrown on a family's barbeque, and then tossed between some of the children in the mob.[29] Ultimately, Theseus slits his own throat after recognizing Strophe, and Hippolytus is left to die as vultures descend and eat his exposed entrails.

Kane does not allow for passive audience witnessing of this dramatic event. Planting actors in the audience implies that we are not only complicit in the violence enacted before us, but that we participate in it as well. Despite the knowledge that the audience turned mob was planted beforehand, the scene positions the "real" audience members in the midst of the violence. As Saunders notes, Kane attempted throughout the production to eliminate the boundaries between audience and actors. The seating was nontraditional in that "seating was dispersed around the theatre, and no single playing space selected."[30] Indeed, even Charles Spencer begrudgingly admitted that the play offered a "visceral impact." He went on to assert, however, "But then it's hard not to shudder when a penis is being severed under your nose and you are in grave danger of being covered in gore."[31]

Although the physical violence of *Phaedra's Love* does not emerge until the end of the play, critics fixated on the atrocities. Paul Taylor of the *Independent* stated, "the last 10 minutes or so move into an area where the atrocity-count begins to reach respectable *Blasted*-like levels as the mob set upon Hippolytus and rape, castration, disembowelment and an orgy of neck-splitting ensues. Kane's highly visceral production seats the audience in the thick of this, so it might be advisable not to wear your best frock." Taylor's rueful critique serves to illustrate the potential perils of stage blood used in excess. The blood spattered on the audience may be seen as a prop that misbehaves, transgressing the lines between the world of the play and the world of the audience. This transgression (and potential staining) can also be read as an intentional breaching of those boundaries designed to implicate the spectator in much the same way as the audience plants and the arrangement of the space.

Saunders describes the extreme violence that is enacted in the final scene as once again reminiscent of Elizabethan or Jacobean tragedy. This violence (and, by extension, the blood) is "outlandish and shocking to the sensibilities."[32] Stefani Brusberg-Kiermeier suggests that *Phaedra's Love* can be seen as "(1) a post-modern re-write (2) in an Elizabethan light (3) of a Roman re-write (4) of a Greek play."[33] Undeniably, *Phaedra's Love* is an exceptionally violent play. Kane herself admitted in her interview with Benedict that she purposefully crafted it in this manner. "She also admits to having a problem with the Greek idea of the violence happening offstage. 'Well, obviously I would,' she laughs. 'I mean, if you're not going to see what happened, why not stay at home? Why pay £10 to not see it? The reported deaths in Seneca are incredibly strongly written, conjuring the image really well, but personally I'd rather have an image right in front of me.'"[34]

Kane's third play, *Cleansed,* opened at the Royal Court in 1998. *Cleansed* is set in a postapocalyptic institution where individuals are being "rehabilitated" (and in many cases destroyed) for their "deviant" desire. Although *Cleansed* is undeniably graphic throughout its twenty scenes, it is imperative to note that it is a highly nonrealistic play. In the original production, the torture wreaked on the bodies was highly stylized. The blood utilized in the production consisted of a series of red textiles. *Cleansed* marked Kane's movement away from representational, illusionistic practices and a move towards an aesthetic that was marked by heightened theatricality.

The torture that Tinker enacts on the bodies of Carl and Rod is the most graphic in terms of its violent extremity. Upon his betrayal of Rod, Carl has his tongue cut out by Tinker. Tinker then forces Carl to swallow the ring he had given Rod. In the next scene with Rod and Carl, Carl attempts to write a message in the mud to Rod: "Say you forgive me." Upon witnessing this, Tinker cuts off Carl's hands. Rod removes his ring from Carl's severed left hand, and a rat begins to eat the severed right hand. In the fourth scene featuring these men, Carl hears a child singing outside the fence and begins a "*dance of love for Rod.*" Tinker again witnesses this act and cuts off Carl's feet. In the final scene between Rod and Carl, Rod states, "There's only now. . . . That's all there's ever been." Yet after making love to Carl, Rod states, "I will always love you. / I will never lie to you. / I will never betray you. / On my life." Then Rod returns his ring to Carl, making him swallow it. Tinker, upon witnessing this last loving exchange between the men asks, "You or him, Rod, what's it to be?" Rod replies, "Me. Not Carl. Me." Tinker then slits Rod's throat.[35]

In the original production of *Cleansed,* the violence enacted upon Rod and Carl was highly stylized. When Carl's tongue was cut out, a red ribbon was pulled from his mouth. This gesture in particular functioned as an explicit citation of Peter Brook's famous production of *Titus Andronicus,* which relied heavily on abstract depictions of extreme violence; described as "devoid of stage blood but flow[ing] with bloody symbolism," Brook's production utilized "scarlet streamers" to indicate blood and mutilation.[36] In *Cleansed,* when Carl's hands and feet were cut off, red sleeves or scarves were pulled over his limbs to look like bloody stumps. The actor playing Carl invested these acts with a realistic response, making those moments all the more viscerally charged for the audience.

The critics responding to the original 1998 production recounted the instances of "theatrical horrors" in which, as Charles Spencer wrote, "limbs are lopped off, tongues severed and penises transplanted with almost merry abandon." Yet, as critics such as Nicholas DeJongh pointed out, "These ghastly incidents—fatal injecting of heroin into an eye, violent amputation of a homosexual's tongue, hands and feet, cutting of a throat, two beatings, one suicide by hanging and a cut throat—are admittedly enacted with stylized artiness." Or, as David Benedict indelicately claimed, "Those expecting a splatter-fest will be disappointed. Everything is done through suggestion, which, of course, is far more harrowing."[37] Indeed, this echoes Brook's own assessment of his 1955 production of *Titus.* He asserted that the production called upon "the most modern of emotions—violence, hatred, cruelty, pain—in a form that, because *unrealistic,* transcended the anecdote and became for each audience *quite abstract and thus totally real.*"[38]

Shortly after completing *Cleansed,* Kane discussed her conscious use of nonrealistic techniques: "I was having a fit about all this naturalistic rubbish that was being written and I decided that I wanted to write a play that could never ever be turned into a film—it could never ever be shot for television; it could never be turned into a novel. The only thing that could ever be done with it was it could be staged, and believe it or not that play is *Cleansed.* You may say it can't be staged, but it can't be anything else either."[39] Undeniably, there is a difference between the use of stage blood in live performance and the use of blood in film or television. Audiences do not run the risk of coming into contact with the blood when the performance is on a screen. A realistic use of blood in the theatre can sometimes be all the more disturbing than in film or television precisely because of the nature of live performance, the physical presence of actors, and the specific challenges inherent in utilizing blood props believably over the course of countless performances. Proximity to the performers in more intimate spaces (such as Soho Rep) can also intensify the experience for audience members. Proximity also complicates the use of blood. With audience members merely a few feet away from the performance space, the execution of stage blood as a prop must be flawless or else runs the risk of destroying the illusion. A more stylized approach may offer a more reliable and predictable use of stage blood as a prop, assuming the audience enters fully into the theatrical contract of that abstracted world.

The use of stylized blood in the original production of *Cleansed* reflected Kane's wishes that the piece remain consciously theatrical. In an interview with Dan Rebellato, shortly before her death, in which Kane discussed her approach to *Cleansed,* she asserted that "I think the less naturalistically you show these things, the more likely people are to be thinking: 'What does this mean? What is the meaning of this act' [r]ather than 'Fucking hell, how did they do that?'"[40] As the description of Sarah Birdhouse's design process for the blood in *Blasted* illustrates, sometimes the question of "how did they do that?" offers a rather complex response. While Kane, especially in her plays written after *Blasted* and *Phaedra's Love,* clearly privileged a more abstract aesthetic, I do not mean to posit a hierarchy or binary between blood use that is abstract and blood use that strives for verisimilitude. Whether the blood props are realistic, over the top, or stylized, they serve many necessary functions within the work of Kane as made manifest in these three productions.

Blood also serves to situate Kane's work within a larger historical framework of those who have previously "summon[ed] up the blood." Sofer describes some props as "haunted mediums" that "ventriloquize an absent, offstage subject."[41] Blood as a prop is also haunted by previous stage incarnations of the stylized or sticky stuff. In his book *The Haunted Stage: The Theatre as Memory Machine,* Marvin Carlson uses the motif of "ghosting" to explain the complex systems of repetition and memory that operate within theatre practice. "[G]hosting," he states, "presents the identical thing they have encountered before, although now in a somewhat different context." Carlson goes on to assert that "Everything in the theatre, the bodies, the materials utilized, the language, the space itself, is now and has always been haunted and that haunting has been an essential part of the theatre's meaning to and reception by its audiences in all times and places."[42] Situated among the "neo-Jacobeans" (as Saunders asserts), Kane's work is haunted by Renaissance artists. *Phaedra's Love* also features the inscriptions of Seneca's Rome, Euripides' Athens, and even Racine's seventeenth-century France (albeit through a disavowal of Racine's more "civilized" approach to the myth). Additionally, her works offer a sense of citationality that draws attention to the genealogy or lineage of certain stylistic choices. *Cleansed* samples, pays homage to, or, at the very least, parallels Brook's *Titus Andronicus,* which then, in turn, draws a connection to the Korean masked dance-drama that inspired Brook.[43] The repeated references to Brook's production in discussions of *Cleansed* illustrate the impossibility of detaching from this fraught history, which, it seems, has been written in blood.

Examining the larger context of Kane's work, including her influences, the shifting critical reception, and the eclectic (if somewhat restricted) production history, further complicates this sense of citationality. Rather than using the blood in Kane's plays as a direct, unproblematized lineage to other practitioners whose practices were similar, it may be more productive to characterize Kane's use of blood as a series of layered inscriptions that bear the bloody tracings of the work that came before and yet also serve as the palimpsests upon which the blood of future works will be written.

Notes

1. Quoted in Jody Enders, *The Medieval Theater of Cruelty: Rhetoric, Memory, Violence* (Ithaca: Cornell University Press, 1999) xx.

2. Rush Rehm, "Festivals and Audiences in Athens and Rome," in *The Cambridge Companion to Greek and Roman Theatre,* ed. Marianne McDonald and J. Michael Walton (Cambridge: Cambridge University Press, 2007), 184. Rehm asserts that "Given their power, the gods may have welcomed protestations of faith, but they required of their worshippers specific actions (rituals). These usually involved blood sacrifice or other offerings, performed in particular places and times as the means to placate them."

3. Enders, *Medieval Theater,* 12. Enders quotes the eighteenth-century aesthetic critic Jean-Baptiste DuBos.

4. Andrew Gurr, *The Shakespearean Stage, 1574–1642,* 2nd ed. (Cambridge: Cambridge University Press, 1987), 166.

5. Richard J. Hand and Michael Wilson, *Grand-Guignol: The French Theatre of Horror* (Exeter: University of Exeter Press, 2002), 3.

6. Andrew Sofer, *The Stage Life of Props* (Ann Arbor: University of Michigan Press, 2003), 2.

7. Ibid., 29.

8. Ibid., 24.

9. Sarah Kane, *Blasted,* in *Complete Plays* (London: Methuen, 2001).

10. Indeed, the critical attack on Kane's work has been likened to the criticism Henrik Ibsen received for *Ghosts* and Edward Bond received for *Saved.* In an interesting turn, many of the critics that responded so ferociously to Kane's work in 1995 recanted their positions and celebrated the play following the 2001 production at the Royal Court, which was part of the Sarah Kane retrospective produced approximately two years after her suicide.

11. Michael Meyer, "Blood Seminar for *Revenger's Tragedy,*" University of North Carolina at Greensboro, Greensboro, NC, Oct. 11, 2008.

12. Sarah Birdhouse, interview by the author, Mar. 29, 2009.

13. Alexis Soloski, "Fall Preview: Sarah Kane's Notorious *Blasted* Finally Receives Its New York Premiere; Eating up Baby." *Village Voice,* Sept. 2, 2008, http://www.villagevoice.com/2008-09-03/theater/fall-preview-sarah-kane-s-notorious-blasted-finally-receives-its-new-york-premiere (accessed Sept. 8, 2008).

14. Birdhouse, interview.

15. Aleks Sierz, *In-Yer-Face Theatre: British Drama Today* (London: Faber and Faber, 2001), 5.

16. Patrick Healy, "Audiences Gasp at Violence; Actors Must Survive It," *New York Times,* Nov. 6, 2008, C1.

17. Mark Blankenship, "Love and Sex: Who's Afraid of Sarah Kane?" *New York Times,* Oct. 5, 2008, AR6.

18. Mark Ravenhill, "Obituary: Sarah Kane," *Independent,* Feb. 23, 1999, 6.

19. Graham Saunders, "*Love Me or Kill Me*": *Sarah Kane and the Theatre of Extremes* (Manchester: Manchester University Press, 2002), 20.

20. David Benedict, "Disgusting Violence? Actually It's Quite a Peaceful Play," *Independent,* Jan. 22, 1995, 3.

21. Kate Bassett, review of *Phaedra's Love,* by Sarah Kane, directed by Sarah Kane, Gate Theatre, London, *Theatre Record* 16, no. 11 (1996): 651.

22. Richard Ouzounian, "Gory Days Are Here Again," review of *Evil Dead the Musical,* directed by Christopher Bond, Diesel Playhouse, Toronto, *Toronto Star,* May 9, 2007, E02.

23. Bryan Reesman, "Buckets of Blood: Signature Theatre's production of *The Lieutenant of Inishmore* Demanded a Gargantuan Cleanup Nightly," *Stage Directions* (February 2009): 28.

24. Saunders, "*Love Me,*" 71.

25. Ken Urban, "Towards a Theory of Cruel Britannia: Coolness, Cruelty, and the 'Nineties," *New Theatre Quarterly* 4, no. 80 (2004): 368.

26. Patti Hadad, review of *Phaedra's Love,* by Sarah Kane, directed by Lorella Loftus and Todd Porter, Austin Renaissance Theatre Company, Austin, TX, *Austin Chronicle,* Sept. 23, 2005.

27. Hillary Fannin, review of *Phaedra's Love,* by Sarah Kane, directed by Jason Byrne, Loose Canon theatre company, Dublin, *Irish Times,* July 9, 2008.

28. Reviews of *Phaedra's Love,* by Sarah Kane, directed by Sarah Kane, Gate Theatre, London, *Theatre Record,* 16, no. 11 (1996): 651–54.

29. Sarah Kane, *Phaedra's Love,* in *Complete Plays* (London: Methuen, 2001).

30. Saunders, "*Love Me,*" 80.

31. Reviews of *Phaedra's Love,* 652.

32. Saunders, "*Love Me,*" 80.

33. Stefani Brusberg-Kiermeier, "Re-Writing Seneca: Sarah Kane's *Phaedra's Love,*" in *Crossing Borders: Intercultural Drama and Theatre at the Turn of the Millennium,* Contemporary Drama in English 8, ed. Bernhard Reitz and Alyce von Rothkirch (Trier, GE: WVT, 2001), 165.

34. David Benedict, "What Sarah Did Next," *Independent,* May 15, 1996, 6.

35. Sarah Kane, *Cleansed,* in *Complete Plays* (London: Methuen, 2001). In a German production in an incredibly ill-thought-out concept, the director actu-

ally attempted to train real rats for use in the play. Needless to say, that was soon abandoned in favor of mechanical stand-ins.

36. Richard Helfer and Glenn Loney, eds., *Peter Brook: Oxford to Orghast* (London: Routledge, 1998), 73.

37. Reviews of *Cleansed,* by Sarah Kane, directed by James Macdonald, Royal Court, London, *Theatre Record,* 18, no. 9 (1998): 563–68.

38. Quoted in Helfer and Loney, eds., *Peter Brook,* 71; emphasis in original.

39. Dan Rebellato, "Sarah Kane: An Appreciation," *New Theatre Quarterly,* 59 (1999): 280–81.

40. Dan Rebellato, i*nterview with Sarah Kane, Nov. 3, 1998,* Department of Drama and Theatre: Royal Holloway University of London; available at http://www.rhul.ac.uk/drama/staff/rebellato_dan/index.html (accessed Feb. 9, 2009).

41. Sofer, *Stage Life of Props,* 27.

42. Marvin Carlson, *The Haunted Stage: The Theatre as Memory Machine* (Ann Arbor: University of Michigan Press, 2003), 7, 15.

43. Helfer and Loney, eds., *Peter Brook,* 73.

Helen's Theatrical *Mêchanê*

Props and Costumes in Euripides' *Helen*

Sarah Powers

Aristophanes' comedies are characterized by a heavy use of props and other theatrical items, such as prominent set and costume pieces. We could think of the giant dung beetle that the heroes ride up to heaven in *Peace* (though some might classify that as stage machinery), Dionysus's lion skin and club in *Frogs*, and the baskets of goodies to which Paphlagon and the Sausage-Seller treat Demos as they fight for his support in *Knights* (and the cascade of the goodies when Paphlagon's basket is overturned, showing how much he has withheld).[1] In *Thesmophoriazusae*, the most memorable use of a prop comes with the wine-skin that Mica, one of the women at the assembly, treats as her baby. In one of the play's climactic scenes, the play's unnamed male main character holds the wine-skin "baby" over the altar and threatens to "kill" it, and the painting on the Telephus vase helps us imagine what this object might have looked like onstage.[2] We have other vase paintings that represent props in other Old Comedies that have not survived, so it seems safe to say that stage properties were an important element of Old Comedy, and as New Comedies often revolved around recognition tokens and other key objects, we can see a continuation of the centrality of props in comedy, even through modern examples of the genre.[3]

However, Greek tragedy and other tragic forms that follow its basic style typically have a very different relationship with props and theatrical paraphernalia. In *Great Reckonings in Little Rooms: On the Phenomenology of Theater*, Bert States has explained what he terms the "rhetorical scenery" characteristic of plays performed in a mostly bare or neutral space, such as those of the Greeks or Shakespeare. States argues that a world in this kind of theatre is created primarily through language and metaphor, which then inflect everything that the audience might see on the stage. He explains, "The very thickness of Shakespeare's world is derived from the way in which poetry triumphs over neutral space." Real objects on this stage may be important, but even these, States contends, tend to be shaped by language and metaphor.[4]

In the context of Greek tragedy, the rich purple fabric that Clytemnestra spreads before Agamemnon in Aeschylus's *Agamemnon* is a prime example of such a heightened or "rhetoricized" prop. Its significance to the scene suggests that it must have been a real object on the stage, but that object is so laden with symbolic value through the play's language that it takes on a much deeper and more complex meaning than an ordinary garment or carpet, even a sumptuous one. In his objection to it, Agamemnon even uses imagery of speech or crying out to describe the inappropriate nature of walking on such ornate fabric: "*chôris podopsêtrôn te kai tôn poikilôn / klêdôn autei*" [literally, "The cry (or 'appellation' or 'omen') of 'foot-wipers' and of 'intricate' (or 'multi-colored' or possibly 'embroidered') shouts in different directions"] (926–27).[5] Not only do Clytemnestra and Agamemnon discuss the cloth at length, then, but Agamemnon even describes the fabric as crying out. Language is thus central to the shaping of this object, and one might even go so far as to suggest that the idea of the object becomes more important than the object itself. This is clearly different from the comic uses of props and costumes that rely so heavily on the materiality and functionality of the objects, as we can see in Aristophanes and others.[6]

Euripides' *Helen* has long been considered a "problem play," and scholars have been especially challenged to classify it generically. Is it a tragedy? A romance? A few have even claimed that it is really a comedy![7] I would like to suggest that long before the "happy" ending, which is in fact characteristic of many Greek tragedies, it is the overabundance, unusual importance, and everyday nature of the theatrical "stuff" (props, costumes, and set pieces) that truly push the play towards the comic end of the spectrum. Undoubtedly, *Helen* is a tragedy by Greek standards, but even to the Greeks (or at least to Aristophanes, as we shall see), the play seemed distinctive for its unusual use of theatrical materials. Through Helen's remarkable use of props and costumes, the play reveals the power of theatre to effect transformations, most directly of characters and stories, but ultimately of theatre itself and its own generic conventions.

Helen opens with a scene that must have been rather surprising to the original audience: drawing on a lesser-known variant of the myth, Euripides places a virtuous and long-suffering Helen in Egypt, claiming asylum on the tomb of the dead king Proteus in order to resist the advances of Theoclymenus, the current king. Helen, it seems, did not go to Troy but rather was swept up by Hermes and dropped off in Egypt for the duration, while a cloud image of herself (an *eidôlon*) went with Paris.[8] Euripides' first major revision to the expected story is to turn Helen, the archetypal unfaithful woman, into a Penelope figure. His second surprise for the audience comes with the entrance of Menelaus: no longer a mighty hero of the Trojan War, this Menelaus is shipwrecked and in rags, having lost his ship, supplies, and many of his men, and he is now reduced to begging for food. The character could be understood as pathetic and embodying the misfortune of a great hero, and so he might seem from the text on the page, but he could also be a rather comic figure, which the action and performance might suggest more strongly. After all, his begging is embarrassingly unsuccessful, as an old servant woman is able to run him off.

After turning these two well-known characters on their heads, Euripides begins to twist the plot into a new direction. The beginning of the play is primarily a series of laments: Helen for her lost reputation, her mother and brothers, the many Greeks and Trojans who have died in a fruitless war, and her current situation as refugee, and Menelaus for his utter lack of resources. After Helen and Menelaus recognize each other, however, they decide not to follow paths that might lead to a more typical tragedy, such as committing suicide or directly attacking Theoclymenus in order to win glory before dying, both of which Menelaus suggests.

Instead, Helen takes control and suggests more practical solutions involving trickery, thus turning the plot into an intrigue: "Listen, if a woman also might say something *sophos*.[9] Would you be willing to be said, by word, to have died, though not having died?" (1049–50).[10] With these lines, Helen takes control of the play, and the plot moves from lamentation and discussion to action. She proceeds to explain her plan, patiently answering each of Menelaus's questions and explaining his role in the scheme. When he asks who she will say told her of his death, she instructs him: "You; and say that you alone escaped death, sailing with the son of Atreus, and that you saw him die" (1077–78). They then agree that his rags will support this story, and Helen instructs him to wait at the tomb while she costumes herself for her role, with a black robe, shorn hair, and bloody cheeks: "And I, having gone into the house, will cut my hair and exchange my white dress for black and run my nails, bloodying of flesh, into my cheeks" (1087–89).

Not only does Helen plan this scheme, but she also gives Menelaus instructions along the way and finds the necessary props and costumes for his roles. Menelaus, of course, supplies his own costume for his first role as a shipwrecked sailor. He has already appeared as a beggar at the gate, and the rags that frighten Helen when she first sees him now cause Theoclymenus's immediate reaction to his appearance: "Apollo! What wretched clothes he has!" (1204). Although Theoclymenus does later confirm the sailor's tale with his all-knowing sister off stage, the more theatrically powerful moment of victory is that in which the rags supply enough proof for him to agree at once to each of Helen's requests, which will supply Menelaus with the accessories that will restore him to his role of hero and king.

Helen tells Theoclymenus that she must bury her husband's body in effigy with robes and such other things as the dead need (1243, 1247). When Theoclymenus asks exactly what he should provide, Helen prompts Menelaus to enter the conversation and list what he needs: "This man knows, but I am inexperienced, having been lucky before now" (1249). With that nudge, Menelaus goes on to request an animal for sacrifice, bedding, armor, fruits of the earth, and a ship with rowers (1255–72). Theoclymenus eagerly promises to provide everything, including clothing and food for the sailor himself, and Helen then instructs Menelaus to go inside, bathe, and put on new clothes: "But you, o wretched man, go inside and wash yourself and put on clean clothes" (1296–97). Helen here addresses Menelaus with yet another imperative and prepares to dress him as becomes a hero.

When Helen returns to the stage after the Chorus's ode to the Mother, she announces to the Chorus that she has cleaned up her husband: "Exchanging robes for the shipwrecked clothing, I [*egô*] have adorned him and given his body washing, fresh water from a dewy river after much time" (1382–84). This report again underscores Helen's control: she has taken care of him herself, as the *egô* [I] emphasizes (1383).[11] Menelaus arrived as a shipwreck, clothed in rags, with a small and bedraggled group of sailors, desperately clinging to a piece of cloud as his booty from Troy. This Menelaus is a beggar at the gates and can only protest weakly in response to the rebuffs of the old woman gatekeeper. Helen has now essentially transformed Menelaus into a heroic king and general who can sail away victoriously from a barbarian land. In his study of the escape tragedies, Matthew Wright explores the relation of this costume change to Menelaus's role change: "As before, his outward appearance reflects, rather than misrepresents, reality: he is about to behave heroically, replaying Troy. His behavior on-board ship . . . seems completely different from before, and perhaps it is, at least partly, due to his new costume. We are bound to ask: does outward appearance *dictate* reality, rather than *vice versa*?"[12] At the very least, costume seems to dictate attitude, and Menelaus, as the messenger later reports, has renewed confidence as he brings reluctant animals onto the ship, conducts the sacrifice, and gives orders to his men. Helen has bathed him, dressed him in fine robes and armor, acquired a ship and crew for him, confirmed that he will have complete authority over the rowers, and restored a real, worthy prize to him in exchange for the *eidôlon:* herself. She has even provided an opportunity for him to reenact the Trojan War and kill more barbarians.

If Helen is instructing Menelaus and controlling the plot as a playwright of sorts, what kind of play is she writing? Certainly it is an escape and a trick, and many have noticed that it is a double of Troy. Charles Segal, for example, sees this doubling as part of a schematic of elements of reality contrasted with elements of appearance. The real Helen, Zeus, Egypt, and the *Odyssey,* among other items in his chart, contrast the *eidôlon,* Hera, Troy, and the *Iliad,* respectively.[13] Segal's list, however, includes one pair that could become another larger schematic by which these elements may be divided. If Helen is reenacting Troy, she is in fact reenacting only the *Odyssey* and rejecting the *Iliad.* Direct martial approaches are ineffective here, and as the gatekeeper tells Menelaus, his military exploits carry no currency in Theoclymenus's land (454). Helen instead follows the model of Odysseus, and her scheme is a clear double of the Trojan horse. By her plan, the Greeks yet again take advantage of the barbarians' gullibility by disguising themselves and luring the enemy into a vulnerable position. Just as the Greeks streamed out of the horse in the middle of the night to ambush the sleeping, unarmed Trojans, Menelaus and his men wait until the ship is at sea and the crew is isolated before they drop the guise of the funeral and slaughter the barbarians. The theatricality of the Trojan horse trick is thus redeployed through Helen's trick, invoking the famous story but replaying it with critical substitutions and revisions.

As she re-creates the *Odyssey,* then, Helen revises several of the roles, beginning with her own. The play's initial image of Helen clothed in white and clinging to a tomb as sanctuary from a would-be lover's advances allows her to figure herself as virtuous and clever, a veritable Penelope. Erich Segal and others note that "Helen has been Penelopized," citing her chastity and loyalty to her husband.[14] In fact, even her trickery evokes the Homeric Penelope: in Book XIX of the *Odyssey,* Penelope explains to her disguised husband her trick of weaving a great shroud by day and unraveling it by night. She even describes the unfinished robe as a *dolos* ("trick" or "stratagem"): "*egô de dolous tolupeuô*" [And I wove my stratagems] (XIX.137). Here, *tolupeuô* can take its literal meaning, "to wind off carded wool into a clew for spinning," or its metaphorical meaning, "to contrive, devise."[15] Penelope's *dolous* are thus both the physical robe she is working and the plan she is devising. How appropriate, then, for Helen, in making a Penelope of herself, to take up not only that figure's chastity, but also her trickery and use of clothing for her schemes.

Also significant for her efforts to revise her role is Helen's degree of control over this intrigue plot. In the traditional Homeric story, Helen is an unfaithful woman and takes much of the blame for the Trojan War, but she is also an object: the prize bestowed on Paris by Aphrodite. Against the tradition of casting Helen in such a negative light, the first-generation sophist philosopher Gorgias argues in his encomium that Helen does not deserve blame for going to Troy, since she cannot be held responsible for the powers of love, the persuasion of words, rape, or the will of the gods.[16] Gorgias may exonerate Helen to some extent, then, but he does so only by presenting her position as one of negligible power and agency. Whether because Zeus wants to lighten the world, or because Aphrodite wants to reward her favorite, or because Paris will persuade or forcibly abduct her, Helen (or an acceptable substitute) must go to Troy.[17]

When Helen has a chance to reenact Troy and revise her role in Euripides' play, therefore, she is able not only to clear her name, but also to assert her own agency by taking firm control of the story. The role Helen writes for herself in this drama is one of chastity, cleverness, and agency. She becomes a combination of Penelope and Odysseus as she gives the instructions for the scheme that will allow her to return home with Menelaus and restore her reputation.

For Menelaus, Helen designs a shifting role. He arrives as a shipwreck and initially can comprehend only direct, martial approaches to their problem, with his impulse being to fight for her (843), to steal a chariot and escape (1039–40), or to ambush and kill the king (1043–44). None of these suggestions is practical, and they contrast strongly with Helen's solution of fiction and trickery. Charles Segal sees a strong antithesis here: "Menelaus' solution to the problem of escape is violent and, as Helen calmly points out, wildly unrealistic. . . . To this death-bent desperation Helen opposes the resiliency of Odyssean guile and adaptability. She plays Odysseus to Menelaus' Achilles."[18] While Helen does convince Menelaus to take part in an Odyssean plan, however, she also makes a space for him to play a military hero in the mold of Achilles. Helen's transformation of Menelaus through his new costume and supplies is also her restoration of him to the role she wants him to play in her *Odyssey,* that of a victorious hero with a worthy prize.

The final role that Helen significantly revises is that of her barbarian captor. Theoclymenus's position is already compromised by his desire for Helen, which clouds his judgment and makes him more trusting of the beloved who promises to renounce her dead husband and accept his proposal of marriage. Furthermore, with his sister Theonoë working against him, Theoclymenus is utterly incapable of resisting Helen's deceptions. Unlike the Trojans, he is not even a worthy adversary. As Anne Pippin Burnett explains, his role as a threatening villain is significantly diminished: "Theonoë's choice of father over brother disarms Theoclymenus so that he cannot properly play even the duped villain of the escape scenes that follow. She deprives him not only of the extraordinary supernatural aid of her warning, but also of his natural defence, his intelligence."[19] The tragic conflict of the Trojan War has been revised into a deception or humiliation farce, complete with a weak, comic buffoon.[20] By ensuring Theonoë's cooperation before deciding to attempt an escape, Helen places Theoclymenus in such a low position that she can safely mock and manipulate him as just such a buffoon, presumably to the delight of a predominantly Athenian audience.

We have now seen the extent to which Helen controls the plot of her trick, and thus of the play, and the importance of props and costumes to this trick by which she reinvents her story and its characters. The question of whether the Greeks themselves might have found such a use of theatrical materials distinctive remains, but while we have no classical Greek Samuel Pepys to give us his personal musings on the performances, we can look to Aristophanes as a receiver. Indeed, Aristophanes mocks Euripides specifically by calling attention to the unusual role of props and costumes in his plays, and *Thesmophoriazusae* even involves an explicit parody of *Helen*.

In Aristophanes' *Thesmophoriazusae,* the unnamed main character, a relative of Euripides by marriage,[21] is apprehended and held for punishment for sneaking into the women's assembly, dressed as a woman, to convince the women not to punish Euripides for his plays' slanders against women. After he is captured, the in-law decides that the best way to attract Euripides to come to his rescue is to reenact one of his plays, and his first choice is "his recent *Helen*" (850).[22] It is an appropriate choice for Aristophanes' parody here, not only for its central element of an escape from a barbarian captor, a nice parallel to the in-law and the Scythian thug who will soon take over guard duty, but also for its overriding concern with theatricality and the physical trappings of the theatre, which *Thesmophoriazusae* shares as well.[23]

As is appropriate for invoking a play so dependent upon a theatrical trick, Euripides' in-law in *Thesmophoriazusae* immediately confirms his idea of enacting *Helen* by noticing that he is already costumed for the role: "Besides, there's already a woman's dress here for me!" (851). After all, one could hardly perform *Helen* without the proper costume. The in-law's female guard, Critylla, however, ultimately does not believe the illusion and refuses to play the role of Theonoë that the in-law attempts to craft for her (897–99). Aristophanes' parody thus works by showing the failure of Euripides' theatrical devices in a "real" crisis.

An even more striking example of Aristophanes' lampooning of Euripides' excessive theatricality comes in the *Acharnians*, which was performed in 425 BC, about thirteen years before *Helen*. In this play, the citizen Dikaiopolis needs to make a persuasive argument to the Chorus, so he decides to go to Euripides to get an appropriately pathetic costume. When Dikaiopolis knocks and refuses to go away, Euripides has himself "ekkyklema-ed" out as he reclines on a couch (409).[24] Dikaiopolis first asks for rags, and he turns down those of Oeneus, Phoenix, Philoctetes, and Bellerophon, before joyfully accepting the Telephus costume. The humor here, of course, is that Euripides has so many ragged costumes to choose from. In fact, he has to instruct his slave on where to find the costume to give to Dikaiopolis: "And it lies above the Thyestean rags, between the Ino ones" (433–34).

Dikaiopolis then begins a long series of requests for props to supplement his costume, including a "little Mysian beanie," a "beggar's cane," a "little basket burned through by a lamp," a "little goblet with a broken lip," a "little bottle plugged with a sponge," and "some withered greenery for my little basket" (439, 448, 453, 459, 462, 469).[25] He gets so caught up in the excitement of the props that he even begins to ask for things that he doesn't need but just wants:

> EURIPIDES: And what need, o wretched one, do you have of this braided basket?
> DIKAIOPOLIS: No need, but I want to have it all the same. (454–55)

Again, Aristophanes is making fun of Euripides for having so many props, and Euripides even complains that Dikaiopolis is going to make off with his entire tragedy: "Man, you'll steal away my tragedy!" (463). Aristophanes is implying that Euripides is unique as a tragedian, and perhaps also ridiculous, because his plays depend so heavily on props and ragged costumes. There seems to be something unusual and a little bit untragic about this.

Further, this sequence of Dikaiopolis asking for a long list of props may in some way be parallel to the sequence of Menelaus requesting the list of supplies from Theoclymenus in *Helen*. In each case, the hero makes a series of demands, each of which is granted, with more or less enthusiasm, by the character who fills the role of the butt of the humor or trick. It is unlikely that Euripides is directly playing off of Aristophanes' scene, especially given the length of time between the two plays, but the similarity between them does suggest that there is some commonality between the plays and their relationships to props and costumes, as each scene involves a sense of building tension or excitement in seeing how many items the hero can extract from the buffoon.

Treating Aristophanes as a receiver of Euripides' plays thus provides a perspective from at least one contemporary Greek that lends support to the theory that Euripides is doing something noticeably unusual, even untragic, with his theatrical apparatus. Stepping back into the play itself, however, also provides an interesting perspective on the nature of the play and Helen's tricks. The play is full of tricks, but the specific words that Helen uses to describe her own trick set it apart from most of the others in the play.

When Helen recounts Zeus's purported rape of Leda, she calls it a "*dolion eunên*" [favorable trick] (20). When she describes the tricks of Aphrodite, she calls the goddess "*dolios*" [tricky or deceitful] and includes in the list of troubles she brings "*apatas*" [deceits] and "*dolia*" [tricks] (238, 1103). Menelaus uses the word "*êpatêmenoi*" [being deceived] to explain to his servant that the gods had deceived them with a cloud (704). When Helen refers to her own tricks, however, she uses the words *mêchanê* [contrivance] and *technê* [art]. She tells Menelaus that he needs a scheme in order to escape from Egypt: "*dei de mêchanês tinos*" [and some scheme is necessary], and after they secure Theonoë's help, she decides that they can now devise a plan to escape together, a "*mêchanên sôtêrias*" [scheme of salvation] (813, 1034). Helen later sets out the two possible outcomes of their attempt: they could succeed, or she could die, "*ên alô technômenê*" [if I am apprehended working my arts] (1091).

While *dolios* is a general adjective meaning "crafty, deceitful, treacherous," usually referring to things, and *apatê* a general word for "trick, fraud, deceit," *mêchanê* and *technê* have an additional sense of something constructed. Liddell and Scott define *mêchanê* as a "contrivance, esp. machine" and secondarily as "any artificial means or contrivance for doing a thing."[26] In the context of a play, the word must also resonate with its use as the theatrical machine by which gods could appear above the stage. The use of *technê* is less explicitly theatrical, but this word too has a sense of something constructed. Its definitions include "art," "skill," "craft," "trade," "means," and "trick," and the word can take either a positive connotation, in the sense of an art or something made with skill, or a negative connotation, in the sense of a wily trick.[27] The latter is more common in poetry than in prose, but both supply examples of each use, and the two senses of the word seem to feed into each other. Euripides therefore has Helen describe her plan with words that suggest artifice, contrivance, and construction in a way that *dolios* and *apatê* do not.[28] Hera, to whom Euripides ascribes responsibility for creating the *eidôlon,* is the only god to whom the words *mêchanê* and *technê* are granted in *Helen,* and the use seems appropriate to distinguish a trick that involves both a mystical, divine metamorphosis and a fictional story involving several characters (610, 930).[29] The divide that emerges is one of simple lies, distinct moments of trickery, and divine metamorphosis on the one hand, and elaborate fictions, extended schemes, and theatrical constructions on the other.

Furthering this distinction, two other uses of *dolios* in the play refer to simpler, more discrete moments of deception. The Chorus tells the story of Nauplius luring Greek ships into rocks by shining a "*dolion . . . astera*" [deceptive star], and the example is part of an ode lamenting the many Greeks who died, deceived by the gods, while fighting for a phantom (1130–31). Again, then, the word is connected to the gods' mysterious and deceptive ways. Finally, the messenger describes Menelaus's attitude toward the ragged sailors he and the group of Egyptians meet on the beach as "*dolion oikton*" (1542). Menelaus's "deceptive pity" is a trick (the means by which Menelaus will bring his sailors onto the ship), but it is a single instance of acting, just one element in Helen's more elaborate plan. This slight nuance between Helen's understanding of her plot as a *mêchanê* or *technê* and the more general uses of the words *dolios* and *apatê* again emphasize the theatricality of her scheme, a sense reminiscent of the playwright's own skill.

Euripides' use of *mêchanê* to refer to Helen's trick thus suggests the constructed and theatrical nature of the plot she directs in tricking the barbarians, and we can therefore see in this play some of the earliest roots of modern comedy. If *Helen* is in some sense comic, I suggest that we can think of it as an early model for the trickster comedies of Greek and Roman New Comedy. By taking control, revising roles, giving orders to her "actors," and providing appropriate props and costumes, Helen anticipates the great metatheatrical tricksters of Plautus. Her theatrical trick of Theoclymenus isn't too far removed from the theatrical tricks of characters like Pseudolus, who deploys a slave, Simia, disguised as a messenger with a sealed letter in hand, in order to trick the pimp Ballio out of a courtesan. Alternatively, we could think of the female tricksters in Plautus's *Miles Gloriosus,* such as Acroteleutium, a courtesan who dresses as a respectable wife in order to trick the braggart soldier into giving up his current girl. Just as Helen deploys theatrical properties and costumes in order to revise her story and play out her own version of Troy, Euripides deploys theatrical materials in order to begin a transformation of theatre itself, laying the groundwork for a new genre.

Notes

1. I invoke this moment because it is particularly dependent upon props. The sequence of each character offering Demos goodies begins at line 1165, and Paphlagon's personal stash is revealed at line 1218. Line numbers are taken from *Aristophanes I,* ed. and trans. Jeffrey Henderson, Loeb Classical Library (Cambridge, MA: Harvard University Press, 1998).

2. The Telephus parody bell-crater, c. 380 BC, Würzburg H5697. Images of this vase are commonly reproduced, and this scene may be found in *The Oxford Illustrated History of Theatre,* ed. John Russell Brown (Oxford: Oxford University Press, 1995), 38, among many other sources.

3. For photos of vase paintings featuring props on the comic stage, see especially the second section of plates in Oliver Taplin, *Comic Angels: And Other Approaches to Greek Drama through Vase-Paintings* (Oxford: Clarendon Press, 1992).

4. Bert States, *Great Reckonings in Little Rooms: On the Phenomenology of Theater* (Berkeley: University of California Press, 1985), 54, 56, 60.

5. Aeschylus, *Agamemnon,* in *Aeschylus II,* ed. and trans. Alan H. Sommerstein, Loeb Classical Library (Cambridge, MA: Harvard University Press, 2008). This translation is my own, and the reference is to line numbers. Sommerstein provides two further ways of rendering the imagery. He translates: "It is cryingly obvious that the words 'embroidered' and 'doormat' don't go well together." He adds a more literal translation in a footnote: "the appellation of 'foot-wipers' and 'embroidered' cries out divergently."

6. It would certainly be incorrect to suggest that props do not appear on the stage in tragedy or that they are insignificant. For a compilation of examples of props in tragedy, see Joachim Dingel, "Requisit und szenisches Bild in der griechischen Tragödie," in *Die Bauformen der griechischen Tragödie,* ed. Walter Jens (Munich: Wilhelm Fink Verlag, 1971), 347–67. Dingel suggests that, contrary to Aristotle's assertion that visible things are unnecessary for tragedy, Greek tragedies do grant significant roles to some props. My argument is that these props are invoked and used in ways that are fundamentally different from those of comic props.

7. Bernard Knox, for example, takes such an approach in his essay "Euripidean Comedy," in his collection *Word and Action: Essays on the Ancient Theater* (Baltimore: Johns Hopkins University Press, 1979), 250–74. Erich Segal also tends to consider some of Euripides' plays to be comedies.

8. Euripides was drawing on a variant of the myth found first in a palinode by Stesichorus, which has not survived, and later in Herodotus.

9. This word is loaded in Euripides. It is often translated "wise," but in the late fifth century, the word was strongly associated with the sophists, traveling teachers who touted their ability to make the unjust argument sound just, as Aristophanes put it in *Clouds* (lines 112–18). The word thus has ambivalent connotations in Euripides, incorporating a sense of trickiness or ruthlessness. "Clever" is probably the best translation, though I prefer to leave it untranslated.

10. Quotations from all plays are cited by line numbers, and all translations from Greek texts are my own unless otherwise noted. Citations from *Helen* are based on the Greek edition by A. M. Dale: Euripides, *Helen,* ed. A. M. Dale (Oxford: Oxford University Press, 1967). I quote the original Greek only when I consider the specific wording particularly significant.

11. In Greek, the verb form itself indicates that the subject is "I," so the addition of *egô* is very emphatic.

12. Matthew Wright, *Euripides' Escape-Tragedies: A Study of "Helen," "Andromeda," and "Iphigenia among the Taurians"* (Oxford: Oxford University Press, 2005), 335.

13. Charles Segal, "The Two Worlds of Euripides' *Helen,*" *Transactions and Proceedings of the American Philological Association* 102 (1971): 574.

14. Erich Segal, "'The Comic Catastrophe': An Essay on Euripidean Comedy," in *Stage Directions: Essays in Ancient Drama in Honour of E. W. Handley,* ed. Alan Griffiths (London: Institute of Classical Studies, 1995), 50.

15. *A Greek-English Lexicon,* comp. Henry Liddell and Robert Scott, revised by Sir Henry Stuart Jones (Oxford: Clarendon Press, 1968), s.v. "*tolupeuô.*"

16. Gorgias, *Encomium of Helen,* ed. and trans. D. M. MacDowell (Bristol: Bristol Classical Press, 1993).

17. Pietro Pucci has further explored the necessity of a substitute in order to displace the blame from Helen. See Pucci, "The *Helen* and Euripides' 'Comic' Art," *Colby Quarterly* 33, no. 1 (1997): 42–75.

18. Segal, "The Two Worlds of Euripides' *Helen,*" 578–79.

19. Anne Pippin Burnett, *Catastrophe Survived: Euripides' Plays of Mixed Reversal* (Oxford: Clarendon Press, 1971), 96–97.

20. Jessica Milner Davis, in *Farce* (New Brunswick, NJ: Transaction Publishers, 2003), outlines four types of farce: deception or humiliation, snowball, reversal, and equilibrium. The deception/humiliation farce centers on the single, unidirectional deception and/or humiliation of the comic villain, building through the course of the play and culminating in his ultimate fall and, usually, his realization that he has been tricked.

21. This character is unnamed in the text but was later given the name Mnesilochus, which is often used in translations of the play. Our clue to the character's relationship with Euripides comes from the term *kêdestês,* which refers to any relation by marriage. (See line 74 for Euripides' reference to the man as his *kêdestês.*) "In-law" is not a perfect way to refer to this main character, but it seems most representative of what we know about him.

22. Aristophanes, *Thesmophoriazusae,* in *Aristophanes III,* ed. and trans. Jeffrey Henderson, Loeb Classical Library (Cambridge, MA: Harvard University Press, 2000). The *Helen* parody continues through line 927, at which point Euripides exits, having been rebuffed by Critylla, the woman on guard duty. After a change of guard, several other parodies of Euripides' plays follow, all used as escape attempts.

23. See especially the scene with Agathon, the tragedian who dresses up in appropriate costumes as he writes his plays, and the process of dressing the in-law as a woman using items borrowed from Agathon (lines 95–279).

24. Aristophanes, *Acharnians,* in *Aristophanes I,* ed. and trans. Henderson.

25. Translation of these items is taken from Jeffrey Henderson's translation in the Loeb edition.

26. *Greek-English Lexicon,* comp. Liddell and Scott, s.vv. "*dolios,*" "*apatê,*" and "*mêchanê.*"

27. Ibid., s.v. "*technê.*"

28. Theoclymenus also describes Helen's trick with the word *technê* after the messenger gives his report: "O wretched me, seized by womanly arts [*technaisin*]" (1621). The only use of *dolios* to describe Helen's trick is the messenger's account that the sailors said, "*Dolios hê nauklêria*" [The voyage is a trick!] (1589). From the sailors' perspective, the sense of *dolios* seems appropriate, and in this case it refers specifically to the sea voyage, rather than to the entire scheme.

29. See lines 31 and following for Helen's relation of Hera's role in her fate. Hera was angry that Paris had chosen Aphrodite in the beauty contest and so turned his reward into an image. Zeus then sent Hermes to whisk Helen off to Egypt.

A Cannonade of Weapons

Signs of Transgression in the Early *Commedia dell'arte*

Kyna Hamill

THE *COMMEDIA ALL'IMPROVISO,* more commonly known as the *commedia dell'arte,* was a mobile art form. Early troupes traveled all over the Italian peninsula, Bavaria, France, and beyond and carried the weight of a certain idea of "Italy" wherever they performed. To reconstruct a sixteenth-century *commedia* performance, we do not have the luxury of full scripted texts; rather we use the architecture of the *canovacci,* or scenarios, along with iconography, letters, contracts, and descriptions of performances. Because it is often studied over only one or two days in a theatre history or survey class, the *commedia*'s history regrettably becomes understood as a conflation of two hundred years of performance tradition.

Thus, the *commedia,* like sixteenth-century Italy, is awash with stereotypes. In Shakespeare's invented Italy, we see the Italian man as a young, honor-seeking, audacious hero. In *Romeo and Juliet,* we meet many "hot-blooded" Italians whose violent passions ruled over political and social codes of conduct. Yet, during this same period on the *commedia* stage, we encounter not hot-blooded Italians mad with passion, but rather grotesque characters sullied by social codes and political turmoil brought on by foreign dominance. This study will examine how the weapon as prop remains an important visible signifier of class transgression in the world of the *commedia* during the period of 1568–1620. As symbols of power, authority, and class, weaponry functioned as an apparatus of social convention. Thus, the comic exaggeration of weaponry by lower classes onstage and in the iconography during this period not only affirms the existence of an established honor system but also mocks it. If, as Andrew Sofer suggests, props "do not just identify, they characterize,"[1] then to use a prop belonging to another class remains a transgressive act of social mobility that must inevitably be controlled.

In her book *The Semiotics of Theater*, Erika Fischer-Lichte defines the idea of signified props in relation to a theatrical character type: "The prop functions as a sign that generates meaning with regard to the subject [character]. . . . [A] prop can thus point to both the general type or character of the stage figure, and to its social status, individual traits, feelings, attitudes, value judgments and view of the world."[2] In addition to signifying a character type, weaponry reveals how a character functions within the boundaries of class. Images rendered between 1570 and 1620 suggest that artistic depictions of *commedia* character types included well-established criteria in their visual appearance: the Inamorato and Capitano each carry a rapier, the Magnifico wields a dagger, while Zanni wears a wooden sword or stick in his belt. We can see that weaponry both individuated the character types in the *commedia* and characterized their social roles on the stage. Thus, wearing a weapon not belonging to one's class signified an obvious social transgression and ultimately distorted the ideals of manly behavior outlined by early writers of honorable conduct such as Baldasar Castiglione.

The period under study encompasses what could be considered the zenith of the major *commedia dell'arte* acting companies as well as the publication of play scenarios.[3] Groundbreaking features of this period as they relate to the *commedia* include: the first documented staging of a *commedia all'improviso* performance in 1568 recorded by Massimo Troiano; renderings of iconographical images depicting the *commedia* created between 1578 and 1621; and Flaminio Scala's collection of scenarios, published in 1611. Moreover, historical events provide a context within which to understand the development of Italy's relationship to violence in the sixteenth and early seventeenth centuries, including: the circulation of published fight manuals by Italian fight masters throughout Europe; the exportation of Italian rapier techniques to foreign students, especially between 1590 and 1599; the perception of the "hot-blooded" Italian by foreign travelers to Italy; and the Spanish occupation of southern Italian city-states between 1560 and 1610. It is also significant to recognize the publishing and translation history of Castiglione's *Il libro del cortegiano* (1528) just prior to this period.[4] Along with the popularity of fight manuals, fashionable behavioral guides determining how the early modern nobleman should behave contributed to the codification of weapon use. Between 1492 and 1570, 145 books devoted to the behavior of the military character and laws of combat and chivalry were printed.[5] Along with foreign editions of Castiglione's *Il libro del cortegiano*, which popularized notions of Italian behavior across Europe, Girolamo Muzio's

Il duello (1550), Giovanni Della Casa's *Il Galateo* (1558), and Stefano Guazzo's *La civil conversatione* (four volumes, 1574–86) all pioneered the transformation of manners from a chivalrous knight into a noble courtier who should be perfect, controlled, and youthful.

Castiglione's idealized courtier also took the possession of weaponry into serious consideration. In the sixteenth century, the weapon was commonly a part of everyday dress for courtly gentlemen whose duty, according to Castiglione, was "to know how to handle expertly every kind of weapon, either on foot or mounted [on a horse]."[6] Castiglione's famous word to embody the characteristics of the courtier, *sprezzatura,* is often translated as "nonchalance." Indeed, the ability to cloak one's art and skill behind an apparent lack of effort became the foundation of all courtly behavior. To Castiglione, the desired quality of *grazia* meant that his courtier should perform every action with effortless refinement. Castiglione also dictated that the kind of outward behaviors the courtier should renounce were those that were typical of street performers and which did not "suit a gentleman." To Castiglione, these included "turning cartwheels, tight-rope walking and that kind of thing."[7] Castiglione's parameters for the appropriate agility of a courtier stipulated that he be gracious at all times. In their grotesque manners and behaviors, Zanni and Pantalone display the antithesis of the ideal courtier.

In his book *The Stage Life of Props,* Andrew Sofer emphasizes the criterion of manipulation of an object over its portability: "a hat or sword remains an article of costume until an actor removes or adjusts it."[8] There is here a kind of *nonchalance* implied in the manipulation of properties; to use the object for its purpose seems congruent with our understanding of the object itself. However, when a character out of his station manipulates a coded object, the act becomes a clear transgression, and all subtlety is lost. If Castiglione's ideals of courtly behavior were meant to codify how a gentleman carried and used his weapon in an understated fashion, then transgression from this ideal would be clearly visible by the properties used onstage.

In the world of the *commedia,* characters seemingly disclose the chaos behind this façade of authority since no authority figure exists onstage. We find no prince or king as in Shakespeare, but rather a mix of grotesque characters in a geographic peninsula with no unilateral authority. Historian Peter Burke suggests that "the relationship happening on and off the [*commedia*] stage is not a simple one, but to foreign visitors . . . it may appear that actors stylize and perhaps exaggerate the gestures current in a given culture."[9] With a cast of characters who represented various regions of the peninsula, the *commedia* not only entertained, but also reinforced the cultural differences among many of Italy's principalities.[10] From the depiction of an "honorable" duel to petty domestic squabbles, violent situations throughout the *commedia* ridiculed the lack of any kind of unilateral authority. Even the Magnifico as "patriarch" became not only the object of ridicule but commonly the victim of violence by his own servants. Breaking from classical form and depicting violence *on* the stage also assumed a kind of complicity with audience members, many of whom had firsthand experience with the manner of violence played out in performance. Troupes depicting "Italian" characters to non-Italian audiences did not overtly seek to transmit cultural stereotypes. I do not suggest either political or malevolent intentions by the players of the *commedia* during this time. Rather, the portrayal of characters representing regional and class identities in "Italy" became easily recognizable to both native and foreign audiences because of codified signs like language, costume, and the weapon.

Sixteenth-century Italian violence, manifested through street brawls, formal dueling, and warfare, seems to have been infamous outside of the peninsula. Shakespeare's Mercutio speaks: "Come, come, thou art as hot a Jack in thy mood as / any in Italy, and as soon moved to be moody, and as / soon moody to be moved."[11] Citations of "hot" Italians can be found not only in drama but in documented appraisals as well. During a trip through Italy in 1608, the English traveler Thomas Coryat recorded the following description of a street fight published as *Coryat's Crudities* (1611): "I observed a thing in Venice that I utterly condemned, that if two men should fight together at sharpe openly in the streets, whereas a great company will suddenly flocke together about them, all of them will give them leave to fight till their hearts ake, or till they welter in their own blood, but not one of them hath the honesty to part them . . . but suffer him to go at random whither he list without inflicting any punishment on him. . . . The like I understand is to be observed in Milan and other cities of Italy."[12]

The late sixteenth-century fencing master Vincentio Saviolo also acknowledged that street violence was not the only cause of alarm. Declaring his anxiety, he wrote in his book *Honor and Honorable Quarrels:* "What is become of the gentilitie and inbredde courtesie of auncient noble Gentlemen? . . . There be certaine undiscreet men [who] . . . stand or go in streets, so to stare and looke men passing by them in the face, as if they woulde for some reason marke them."[13] Violence, it would seem, occurred not only to defend one's honor but also for no reason at all. The reputation of these hot-blooded Italians to foreigners resulted from the circumstances of a class of men who apparently had the skills to fight but lacked a legitimate outlet to practice them. Although Castiglione's courtier needed to know every sort of weapon, he was meant to "accomplish the exploits . . . in view of all the noblest and most eminent men of the army, and above all, in the presence, or if possible under the very eyes of the prince he is serving."[14]

Although documented records of the players' proficiency with weaponry is lacking, we do have record of a bizarre incident in 1608, involving a scuffle between an ill-mannered French gentleman and a hot-tempered player from the *Accesi* troupe invited to perform at the Hotel de Bourbon.[15] The troupe later offered public performances to paying customers under the patronage of the Gonzaga family from Mantua.[16] From a notice by the Mantuan agent at the French court to the Duke of Mantua, March 19, 1608:

> A French gentleman, of noble descent and a close relative of M. le grand Ecuyer, went to a comedy, and gave Battistino, a smack, in lieu of the money requested by him at the door, then he hustled past [the actor] and went inside. The player followed him in complaining of the slap and requested the entrance fee once again. At this, the gentleman said "I have paid you in the money you deserve." At that, Battistino, full of rage, advanced on him and said "If that is the case, I owe you this," and at the same time, he punched [the Gentleman] in the nose so hard that it began to bleed. The gentleman drew his sword, as did many other men, but the player managed to save himself with the help of other Italians who were there. Two nights later, the aforementioned gentleman, with a well-armed gang of thugs, went to the player's house to kill the poor man. They all pretended to be from the Royal Guard. They were recognized, however, and since the exit of the staircase and the doors of the rooms were closed, Battistino escaped by another exit with the help of the landlord. He had been well-prepared, however, having a pistol in one hand and a sword in the other, to save his skin. . .[17]

I draw attention to the weapons the player Battistino armed himself with: "having a pistol in one hand and a sword in the other." He carried not one but two weapons; and though he never actually fought the Frenchman, the implication is that he *could* have. The story itself unfolds like a plot from a *commedia* scenario, and the formula suggests a kind of established *lazzi:* if one weapon was good, two would be better, and a cannonade of weapons would be the epitome of comedy. I borrow this word "cannonade," or "*cannonate,*" from Castiglione, who, ever the gentleman, remained critical of men who overloaded themselves with weapons: "He should not behave like those who are always quibbling and arguing over points of honour, and when they have the choice of weapons, select those which can neither put nor prick, arm themselves as if they had to face a cannonade, and, thinking it enough if they are not defeated, retreat all the time and keep on the defensive, giving proof to utter cowardice, and in this way making themselves the sport of children."[18] In order to establish that a cannonade of weapons may have been a set piece of comic stage business meant to satirize long-held conventions of Castiglione's *Il libro del cortegiano,* I would like to revisit three of the most important documents we have about the early *commedia dell'arte.* These include Massimo Troiano's description of a *commedia all'improviso* in 1568; an image from the *Recueil Fossard,* a catalog of prints from the 1570s; and Flaminio Scala's *Il teatro delle favole rappresentative* (1611), a collection of actor-devised scenarios which, to quote Kenneth Richards and Laura Richards, "gives more importance to movement and gesture than to language."[19]

I suggest that the convention of overloading weapons for comic effect may have been sourced from Castiglione's principles of gentlemanly conduct, which were well known by the end of the sixteenth century. That weapons could so strongly signify class and authority in Italian society implies that to use them onstage would be a highly visual code. Furthermore, the weapons used onstage would not be imitated "props" but objects moved from the real world to the stage world, thus carrying all social signification with them. To be burdened by a cannonade of weapons suggests an exaggerated indication of the codes of manly conduct, and a criticism of Castiglione's ideals by a class of men who could never achieve them.

The convention of a cannonade of weapons can be seen as early as 1568 when Duke Albrecht of Bavaria requested Massimo Troiano da Napoli, his master of music, to provide a comedy in the style of the Italian *commedia all'improviso* for his son's marriage. The ceremony took place in Munich on February 22 and on March 8, and *La cortegiana inamorata* was performed before an audience of nobility from all over Europe.[20] In his description of the celebration, published in Munich in 1568 and Venice in 1569, Troiano gave a detailed account of the performance.[21] We learn that Troiano not only organized the event but participated as a player as well. While this account remains the first documented description of a *commedia* performance, Richards and Richards and M. A. Katritzky have pointed out the error in assuming that it was enacted by an Italian troupe. In fact, the scenario for *La cortegiana inamorata* was presented by Troiano, Orlando di Lasso, the master of singing, and their colleagues at court, not by a professional Italian troupe.[22] Richards and Richards clarify: "The description does not serve as a guide to professional performance, but clearly indicates that by 1568 acting *all'improviso* was known beyond Italy, and was defined as performance 'in the Italian manner.'"[23]

Fortunio, Troiano's mouthpiece in the description, explains the details of the play: "This evening a comedy was performed in the Italian manner *all'improviso*, in the presence of all the most illustrious ladies, and notwithstanding most who attended did not understand what was said."[24] Troiano's attempt to authenticate the performance "in the Italian manner" is clear, since he cast the roles among his Italian colleagues and had the characters speak in a Tuscan dialect. Even if some of the spectators had never been to Italy, the characters' behavior stood far enough apart from the norms of Bavarian society that the action and setting onstage would have been understood as satirizing Italian and not Bavarian life.

In the scenario, Pantalone and Zanni meet on the street after many years. Pantalone reveals to Zanni his love for Camilla. To woo her, Pantalone dispatches Zanni to offer her some chickens, but when Zanni meets her, he too falls in love with her. By act 3, Pantalone has exchanged clothes with Zanni thinking that Camilla has requested to see him "in the manner and style Zanni will advise."[25] This action initiates a comic interlude where Zanni, dressed in his master's clothes, and Pantalone, dressed as his servant, instruct each other on how to act according to each other's social standing. They then try to sneak into the house to see Camilla, whom they both love. Her guardian, Polidoro, discovers Pantalone and, in the words of the narrator, Fortunio, "[Polidoro] was annoyed at Pantalone and seizing a stick gave him, if I remember rightly, more than he deserved, to the accompaniment of bursts of laughter from the spectators."[26] Upon hearing the whacks, Zanni hides by tying himself into a sack, but is beaten by the Spanish captain, who is also there to woo Camilla, and who has tripped over the sack. As Fortunio describes it, "[The Spaniard] picked himself up in a towering rage and undid the sack, pulled out Zanni, dusted his bones with a good beating, and chased him off the stage."[27] As a measure to defend their honor, Zanni and Pantalone later appear fully laden with weapons. Fortunio continues: "Pantalone appeared equipped in unbuckled armour, followed by Zanni who had two muskets on his shoulder, eight daggers in his girdle, a target and a sword in his hand, and a rusty helmet on his head. . . . [Then] they practiced some of the strokes with which they would have you believe that they would dispatch their enemies."[28]

The two fools are, of course, unsuccessful and spend more time arguing about who will strike the first blow, or which weapon to use when the time comes to draw—a direct swipe at Castiglione's courtier, who would have known what to do in such a question of honor. Though Pantalone and Zanni become reluctantly involved in the violence, an at-

Plate from the *Recueil Fossard*, ca. 1570, by unknown artist, © Nationalmuseum. Used by permission of the National Museum of Fine Art, Stockholm.

tempt to defend their honor satirizes a gentleman's right to defend himself against an offense. Here, we have two characters without the social right to maintain their honor, but attempting to claim it by overburdening themselves with weapons—clearly not their own.

In the figure from the *Recueil Fossard* collection—a series of plates which offer a partial plot of a scenario—we see a similarly overburdened Harlequin who carries too many weapons to be effectively used.[29] The captions in the voice of Harlequin read from left to right:

> Since I have as a helmet this trusty iron pot,
> And this armature on my back, mounted on my lady donkey,
> Like Hercules I want to attack all of hell,
> In support of the beauty of my mistress.
>
> The beautiful Francisquine is my sweetheart and my right,
> She is my happiness, she is my only hope,
> To have her I will use my friends and my means,

After which, the cutting edge of the sword will not fail,
As a wandering knight of the round table
In love with a nice piece of ass, so that one would say
That there is no one like Harlequin to triumph in the world.[30]

In a Don Quixote–like exploit, not only does he wear a pot on his head, but he also overloads himself with a medieval lance, a sword at his side, as well as a breastplate that appears to be backwards. He also rides a *female* donkey (*ânesse*) rather than a horse. Clearly, the spectacle of Harlequin going off to fight for a woman functions in opposition to Castiglione's courtier whose motives for battle should be honor and the protection of the prince, not a grotesque attempt at chivalry. Harlequin's ridiculous exhibit distorts all efforts at honor by depicting a fool on an inflated mythological errand in an outdated medieval context. In subsequent plates from the *Recueil Fossard*, Harlequin goes on to steal Horatio's clothing and weaponry and will eventually be exposed in his deceit. As we shall see, the disclosure of attempts at power and authority by the lower classes must be revealed by the end of the scene. Only in the restitution of arms can the satire of the weapon's symbolic power be temporarily permitted.

Finally, and perhaps of particular interest to this discussion of props, I cite the first of Flaminio Scala's scenarios: Day 1—*Li duo vecchi gemelli, or The Two Old Twins*. Each of Scala's fifty scenarios includes a summary of the plot, a cast of characters, and a list of properties to be used in the playing of each scene. Here, we can find inventories of lanterns, costumes, drinking and eating utensils, foodstuffs, and of course weapons, alongside valuable information about special effects like "a bladder of blood" (Day 38) and "blood and paste to fake a wound" (Day 29).[31] Aside from the necessary vigilance regarding their authenticity as exact scripts, we can assume, as historian Cesare Molinari does, that Scala's scenarios are representative of *commedia* performance by portraying stock comic situations with few varying themes.[32] In *Li duo vecchi gemelli* (Day 1), the required properties include, among others, "a stick for beating people" and "weapons for Pedrolino and Arlecchino," the two comic servants. The foreshadowing of a fight occurs when Capitano Spavento enters ranting because Graziano will not give his daughter, Flaminia, in marriage. While Capitano's servant, Arlecchino, "blusters as well," Pedrolino steps in and slaps Arlecchino. Capitano draws his sword, and everyone runs away. Arlecchino later gets his revenge by beating Pedrolino with a stick. In the inevitable scene where Pedrolino must also get revenge, to "defend his honor" for the offense, he arrives "loaded down with weapons."[33] Meanwhile, Capitano has taken offense because Orazio wants

Flaminia for his own wife. Although both Capitano and Arlecchino arrive together "loaded with weapons" for their simultaneous duels, Capitano is dissuaded from fighting, while the whole cast of characters observes as "the fully armed Arlecchino, is quickly assaulted by Pedrolino and all weapons are flourished" before the others get involved to make peace.[34] Since both servants want to marry Franceschina, the fight becomes a cocklike battle between two fools who each wield too many weapons to be able to fight properly. Since we have only the outline of a fight, it would seem the players were meant to fill in the action of the fight according to their own skill and ability. In the scene, Pedrolino eventually wins Franceschina's hand, while Arlecchino returns to his lowly position as second servant.

As each of these battles unfolds with characters burdened by a cannonade of weapons, we can see how the power systems remain temporarily reversed onstage. We see servants dress and fight with the weapons of gentlemen, although they exceed the limits of honor by exaggerating the ideals of an honorable quarrel as proposed by Castiglione. It is a backwards world, and the only way to return to the normal scheme of things is to offer punishment toward those who try to invert the social hierarchy by using weapons beyond their class. The return to normal becomes a crucial device because the possession of a rapier or sword by one not worthy of honor must always be seen to be short-lived. If, according to Castiglione, the possession of arms signifies the reputation of a gentleman, then overloading one's self is a serious transgression. Punishment and humiliation remain the only tactic to keep the servant from entering the class of men allowed to truly defend their honor with weapons. Thus, to use an object assumes one's right to use it. Authority, then, on the *commedia* stage is not the king or the prince, but the apparatus of maintaining one's place in the social hierarchy. Here, the weapon as prop in the early *commedia* remains a "loaded" object of class subjectivity.

Notes

1. Andrew Sofer, *The Stage Life of Props* (Ann Arbor: University of Michigan Press, 2003), 12.

2. Erika Fischer-Lichte, *The Semiotics of Theater*, trans. Jeremy Gaines and Doris L. Jones (Bloomington: Indiana University Press, 1992), 108–9.

3. Kenneth Richards and Laura Richards, *The Commedia dell'arte: A Documentary History* (Oxford, UK: Blackwell, 1990), 55.

4. Translated into Spanish (1534), French (1537), English (1561), and German (1566). See Peter Burke, *The Fortunes of the Courtier: The European reception of*

Castiglione's Cortegiano (University Park, PA: Pennsylvania State University Press, 1995), appendix 1 (158–62).

5. For a further discussion of military book printing in Venice, see J. R. Hale, *Renaissance War Studies* (London: Hambledon Press, 1983), 429–60.

6. Baldasar Castiglione, *The Book of the Courtier,* trans. George Bull (London: Penguin, 1976), 61.

7. Ibid., 63.

8. Sofer, *Stage Life of Props,* 12.

9. Peter Burke, "The Language of Gesture in Early Modern Italy," in *A Cultural History of Gesture,* ed. Jan Bremmer and Herman Roodenburg (Ithaca, NY: Cornell University Press, 1991), 75.

10. Hannibal S. Noce also examines the representation of nation on the *commedia* stage, although he focuses more on language in the eighteenth century. See "Aspirations for an Italian National Theatre and the *Commedia dell'arte,*" in *The Science of Buffoonery: Theory and History of the Commedia dell'arte,* ed. Domenico Pietropaolo (Toronto: Dovehouse Editions, 1989), 77–84.

11. William Shakespeare, *Romeo and Juliet,* ed. John E. Hankins (Baltimore: Penguin, 1961), 3.1.5–13.

12. Thomas Coryat, *Coryat's crudities hastily gobled vp in five moneths trauells in France, Sauoy, Italy, Rhetia co[m]monly called the Grisons country, Heluetia aliàs Switzerland, some parts of high Germany, and the Netherlands . . .* (Glasgow: James MacLehose, 1905, facsimile of 1611 edition), 2:413–14.

13. Vincentio Saviolo, *Honor and Honorable Quarrels* (reprinted in Alfred Hutton, *The Sword through the Centuries* [Mineola, NY: Dover, 2002]), 76).

14. Castiglione, *Book of the Courtier,* 115.

15. This is the only example I have come across suggesting that actors from the *commedia* participated in real combat. The incident also implies that actors had to occasionally partake, firsthand, in the culture of violence. See A. Baschet, *Les comédiens italiens à la court de France sous Charles IX, Henry IV, et Louis XIII* (Paris: 1882; Geneva: Slatkine Reprints, 1969), 152.

16. Richards and Richards, *Commedia dell'arte,* 65.

17. Baschet, *Les comédiens italiens,* 170, author's translation. This passage has also been translated into English by Richards and Richards, *Commedia dell'arte,* 270, although their date of the letter is incorrect.

18. Castiglione, *Book of the Courtier,* 62.

19. Richards and Richards, *Commedia dell'arte,* 226.

20. This performance has been discussed in a number of sources, most recently by Susan Maxwell in "A Marriage Commemorated in the Stairway of Fools," *Sixteenth Century Journal* 36, no. 3 (Fall 2005): 717–42. See also Gary Fisher, "The Use of Voices and Instruments at a Sixteenth-Century Wedding Feast," *Choral Journal* 35, no. 1 (August 1994): 9–12; M. A. Katritzky, "The Diaries of Prince Ferdinand of Bavaria: *Commedia dell'arte* at the Wedding Festivals of Florence (1565) and Munich (1568)," *Italian Renaissance Festivals and Their European Influence,* ed. J. R. Mulryne and Margaret Shewring (Lewiston, NY: Edwin Mellen Press, 1992); and M. A. Katritzky, *The Art of the Commedia:*

A Study in the Commedia dell'arte 1560–1620 with Special Reference to the Visual Records (Amsterdam: Rodopi, 2006), 44–79.

21. Massimo Troiano, *Dialoghi ne' quali si narrano le cose più notabili fatte nelle Nozze dello Prencipe Guglielmo VI, Duca di Baviera* (Venetia, 1569). The description of the performance has been translated in Richards and Richards, *Commedia dell'arte,* and in Kathleen Marguerite Lea, *Italian Popular Comedy: A Study in the Commedia dell'arte, 1560–1620,* 2 vols. (Oxford: Clarendon Press, 1934).

22. Richards and Richards, *Commedia dell'arte,* 48. See also M. A. Katritzky, "Lodewyk Toeput: Some Pictures Related to the *Commedia dell'arte,*" *Renaissance Studies* 1, no. 1 (1987): 73.

23. Richards and Richards, *Commedia dell'arte,* 49.

24. Quoted in Richards and Richards, *Commedia dell'arte,* 49.

25. Quoted in Richards and Richards, *Commedia dell'arte,* 50.

26. Quoted in Lea, *Italian Popular Comedy,* 1:10.

27. Quoted in Lea, *Italian Popular Comedy,* 1:10.

28. Quoted in Lea, *Italian Popular Comedy,* 1:10. Also, a "target" is a round shield.

29. For a discussion on reconstructing the sequence, see Katritzky, *Art of the Commedia,* 107–114.

30. Translations by the author and Jennifer Philips, Ph.D.

31. Flaminio Scala, *Il teatro delle favole rappresentative,* ed. Ferruccio Marotti (Milan: Borgonuevo 2, 1976). See also Richard Andrews, ed. and trans., *The Commedia dell'arte of Flaminio Scala* (Lanham, MD: Scarecrow Press, 2008).

32. Cesare Molinari, "Actor Authors of the Commedia dell'arte: The Dramatic Writings of Flaminio Scala and Giambattista Andreini," trans. M. A. Katritzky, *Theatre Research International* 23, no. 2 (July 1998): 145.

33. The original Italian reads: "tutto carico s'armi, per vendicarsi delle bastonate ricevute da Arlecchino" (Scala, *Il teatro,* 1:27–28).

34. The original Italian reads: "tutto armato: vede Arlecchino, subito l'assalta, mettendo mani all'armi. Arlecchino il medesimo. Tutti mettono di mezzo e li fanno far pace" (Scala, *Il teatro,* 1:27–28).

Adding Some "PEP" ("Proto-Expressionistic Props") to the Swedish Stage

Strindberg's Property Usage and His Intima Teater

Christopher J. Mitchell

"SEEK . . . A SMALL theme exhaustively treated . . . searching but short," exhorted August Strindberg in articulating the guiding principles of his groundbreaking "Intima Teater" project of the early twentieth century.[1] While the intimacy and complexity of the characterization in plays like the *To Damascus* series often garner the lion's share of attention from theatre historians, in the plays written specifically for this theatrical project, judicious and spare property usage was a key element to their dramaturgy—a philosophy that carried over into production. These objects—carried or worn—held great power in the characters' worlds, often projecting the characters' tormented mental states or parading their past sins in a proto-expressionistic fashion. Using textual evidence from the four Chamber Plays—*Storm, The Burned House, The Ghost Sonata,* and *The Pelican*—this paper will illustrate how property usage was extraordinarily important to this early salvo in the development of the modern nonrealistic theatre.

The Intima Teater: "Avoid All Ostentation"

Strindberg made a few abortive attempts over the years to start a theatre devoted to the staging of his work, but it wasn't until the last decade of his life that the dream was realized with the help of the young director August Falck.[2] The rather claustrophobic warehouse space on

Norra Bantorget in Stockholm "made it difficult to create illusions of depth,"[3] but was well suited to a theatre of "no elaborate apparatus"[4] as Strindberg had hoped for. Chronically underfunded, and oftentimes supplemented with props culled from Strindberg's own apartment,[5] the theatre nevertheless got off the ground in 1907 with one of his Chamber Plays written directly for it, *The Pelican.* This piece was so poorly received by the critics that Falck was forced to hastily create a production of the more successful *Miss Julie* to raise capital. Another Chamber Play, *The Burned House,* suffered a similar fate. It wasn't until *Storm* premiered at the end of that year that the reviews were warmer. This did not signal a consistent upward trend, for critical bewilderment returned with the following year's debut of *The Ghost Sonata,* causing that play to be removed after twelve performances.[6] While discouraged by the hostile reception coming from a critical coterie that was no doubt schooled in more lavishly set productions, such as those performed elsewhere in Stockholm, Strindberg nonetheless was unrelenting in his demands for the theatre; he dismissed the idea of elaborate furniture and props on the fear that they would "undo [the] new fabric" that he and Falck were creating.[7] "Don't encumber the stage with props and furniture!" he exhorted Falck in a letter of April 1908 (one of many issuing directives to the young man).[8] He elaborated on the rationale for this a month later: "By keeping the scenery simple, what matters emerges: the character, role, speech, expression, gestures."[9] Falck concurred, wishing the theatre to "be the home of the art of suggestion, to open up a perspective for the imagination, and so make the spectator himself participate in the dramatic process." Symbolistic and what would later be called expressionistic techniques were used to highlight areas of the stage in which imagination could reign and altered states could be presented. One example was the usage of "drapes rather than a realistic interior" for a production of *The Father.*[10] While several of his more naturalistic plays such as *The Father* were retrofitted to suit Strindberg's new staging philosophy, it was the Chamber Plays that best fit—and this is discernible directly from the dramatic text.

Ghostly Props and Not-So-Hidden Presences

Much of the glue that binds the four so-called Chamber Plays together is the well-timed appearance of properties that either carry symbolic power for the characters or, more expressionistically, convey dreamlike presences—usually of some character that had impact on the lives of the dramatis personae in the past. More pointedly, these presences often seem to exist so as to serve as persistent reminders of past injustices; but in one case (*Storm*) they become a catalyst to positive action. Sometimes the actual apparition appears (to some); but more often it is only the prop that manifests.

The former case manifests in arguably the best known of the four plays, *The Ghost Sonata* (what Strindberg calls "Opus Three" of the series). The play opens with the appearance of a ghostly Milkmaid, who is seen only by the Student protagonist.[11] The Student enters, battered and bruised from assisting with the wounded and dead in the "terrible accident"[12]—a house collapse—that transpired the previous evening, and his only desire is for the drinking cup that hangs from the water fountain. The cup becomes the center of a miniature power struggle with the Milkmaid, in that the Student sees her using the cup to drink from, requests its usage, and finds the Milkmaid to be rather reluctant to give it up. According to the stage directions, the Milkmaid is frozen by terror at the exchange, perhaps due to the Student's haggard appearance.[13] After the Student gives an apologia for this, she relents, and even goes so far as to acquiesce to the Student's request for her to wet a clean handkerchief and place it over his "inflamed" eyes.[14] While all of this is transpiring, the seemingly omnipresent Old Man (Hummel) watches in fascination, apparently of a Student interacting with thin air—whether he sees the cup is not one hundred percent clear[15]—but when the conversation returns to the topic, the Student asks Hummel if he saw a Milkmaid handing him the cup. Hummel's response is terrified: "Milkmaid?!"[16] The effect is complete when the Milkmaid reappears, for Hummel joins the Student in being able to see her, and it is clear why she is there. According to the stage directions, "She stretches her arms above her head like a drowning person and stares fixedly at the Old Man. The Old Man sits down and shrivels up in terror,"[17] suggesting that he was implicit in her death. This is confirmed later by the Colonel's manservant, Bengtsson, who fills in the detail that Hummel lured the girl onto thin ice in order to drown her, for she was witness to a crime he committed.[18]

The ghostly props and presences do not end there; it is not long into the Student-Hummel exchange when another presence manifests itself: a Dead Man, wrapped in a winding sheet, emerging from the door of the Colonel's house following his funeral. Once again, only the Student can see him—this ability is attributed to his being a "Sunday child"[19]—and the Student observes the apparition looking up at the flag flying in tribute to the man, visually echoing the sheet he's wearing. This time, however, the Old Man feels he has power over the apparition, revealing knowledge that the man was a "benevolent scoundrel" who served the poor but embezzled a large sum of money from the state. Nevertheless, there is fear of the power of the Dead Man's presence, for the Old

Man expresses pity for those who failed to send a tribute card for the man.[20] Interestingly, the sheet costume-prop reemerges in another form: wrapped around the character in the closet called "the Mummy," who is the lady of the house, driven insane by years of anguish. The Mummy is reduced to cooing like a parrot to the humans that interact with her, but rediscovers her voice when her former lover/abuser, the Old Man, enters the house. Instead of being actually dead, the Mummy wishes she were: "Oh God, why can't we die? If only we could die!" she cries in anguish over the twisted mess that is her household.[21]

One might offer the argument that the third major ghost- (or death-) prop in the play is more a set piece, but it does get its share of movement on the part of the actors: the death screen, a black-colored Japanese device that is used to signal the impending demise of a terminal patient—that the person is becoming a ghost.[22] The screen is used twice: once when the Old Man is publicly chastised for his past sins and is himself reduced to babbling à la the Mummy, and again when the Young Lady, the object of the Student's admiration for her beauty and suffering, announces her own death in the face of her overwhelming anguish.[23] In both cases, Bengtsson, who usurps the power from the Old Man, is called upon to administer the screen.

In the other three Chamber Plays, lesser known to the English-speaking theatre world, props are not used by apparitions (or soon-to-be apparitions) but nevertheless exert a ghostly power that transforms the characters' lives. In Opus Four, *The Pelican,* about a widowed mother and her dysfunctional relationship with her children and Son-in-Law, the centerpiece prop becomes a letter penned by the dead father and addressed to his Son, containing his apologia. The widowed Mother, who constantly pleads poverty and long-suffering in the wake of a jealous and spendthrift husband's ways, reacts violently to the letter's content, calling it "Lies, all of it lies!"[24] The dead Father's plea is that he was verbally abused to the point of despair and death, which the Mother denies, but his plea is nevertheless confirmed by the daughter's husband, who is the ally/ostensible lover of the Mother.[25] The letter is later discovered torn up—torn by the Mother, not surprisingly—and ready to be used as kindling for the fireplace but is rescued by the Son,[26] who himself is deep in despair over his father's fate. The letter forces him to "wake up" but further plummets him into the abyss and causes his sister, Gerda, to feel likewise.[27] In the aftermath of this, Gerda sees the need for "justice done," but the Son goes further, citing the need for "revenge."[28]

As if the presence of the letter weren't strong enough, the action is punctuated by the arrival of a strong wind, which blows about all of the Father's papers (including the letter) in the beginning of the climactic final scene, in which the "father's presence" seems to announce the impending demise of the Mother, who, in the face of a fire that breaks out in the house, chooses to jump out the balcony window rather than burn.[29] The wind had appeared previously in the play, having animated the papers in a similar fashion, so as to make the symbolism clear.[30]

While arguably more a set piece (as is *The Ghost Sonata*'s death screen), the rocking chair has a transformative power: the occupants of it seem to channel the spirit of the dead father. First, the Son-in-Law sits in it. He is already resentful of being jilted by the Mother, whose promises of money and security to him in the wake of the Father's death seem to have evaporated. Holding a "heavy cane" as he sits, he speaks commandingly, if bitterly, to the Mother, causing her to remark, "How much you're like the old man now . . . !"[31] Later, the Son sits in it and, in it, finds the strength to confront the Mother for what he feels were the injustices he suffered at her hands—even going so far as to assail the Mother for failing to breast-feed him as a child.[32] The Mother, prior to her suicide, acknowledges the power of the chair: "The chair drives me insane. It always sounded like two knives being whetted when he rocked in it . . . and hacked at my heart."[33]

Continuing the fire theme is Opus Two of the series, *The Burned House*. In this case, however, the fire has already occurred, having burned down an apartment building, causing endless speculation among the gossipy residents of the neighborhood. Suspicions abound, particularly surrounding (interestingly, again) a Student; and an investigation proceeds, dredging up in the ashes the reminders of past "sins" in convenient theatrical prop form. As the exchange between the Dyer and the Stranger, who has returned from a long sojourn in America, wryly observes:

> THE DYER: [*happy*] Are you haunting the ruins?
> THE STRANGER: Ghosts feel at home in ruins . . .[34]

The Stranger extracts from the "ghostly" ruins a number of objects: the student's books, one of which was stolen from the Stranger as a youth and caused a maid to be dismissed in false suspicion; a piece of a frame from a "family portrait" of the Stranger's "fabulous" grandfather, who was a "smuggler who sat in the stocks"; and even the base of a dining-room table, whose composition was thought by the Stranger to be much more valuable ebony and in fact was maple, stained with dye. He finds even more power-laden objects subsequently: a dining-room clock which "kept time for two generations" but "used to stop when somebody died, but when [he] died [left for America], it kept on going," he notes bitterly.[35] In perfect expressionistic form, the object crumbles to dust upon being handled, evaporating as if part of a dream or flashback, causing him to remark: "Nothing survives our touch—nothing! Vanity, vanity!" Waxing poetic, he climaxes with the unearthing of a globe, which he eulogizes by saying it represented "tiny Earth: densest and heaviest of planets—the most oppressive. . . . Hard to breathe your atmosphere, and hard to bear you. . . . Your symbol is the cross—but it could have been a cap and bells or a straitjacket. World of illusion and lunatics."[36]

This play is slightly more props-heavy than its Chamber Play brethren, but none seem to be ill chosen, or lacking power. Like the spruce greens used as a funeral symbol in *Ghost Sonata,*[37] wreaths pop up often in this play in memoriam to past presences.[38] A lamp, which the Student uses to read his books by, becomes the instrument of destruction of the building—but also of revelation of its secrets thereafter.[39] And, like the powerful costume-props of *Ghost Sonata* (the sheet) and *Pelican* (the cane), the Stranger here symbolically offers a tiepin to the harrowed Student, not so much for the latter's pleasure but rather for the former's: "Pretty, isn't it? . . . there are moments when I'd like to see it on someone else's tie, and admire it."[40] The moment reads like a passing of the torch from the older generation to the more youthful, but, in true Strindbergian fashion, the youth are not without deep cynicism about life to come.[41]

The simplest of the lot, props-wise, seems to be the first opus, *Storm,* in which once again the power of memories threatens to intervene in lives. Set in the dwindling days of the magical Swedish summertime, the action revolves around an older Gentleman, a retired civil servant who is reflecting on his life. All activity centers near an apartment building—"the Quiet House," as it's called—in which the Gentleman feels "immobilized . . . rooted . . . by memories."[42] Conflict ensues when the Gentleman's former wife, Gerda, returns in the wake of displeasure with her current husband's reckless gambling-house ways and concern for the effects on her child,[43] finding that the Gentleman still pines for her memory.[44] With the help of their mutual acquaintance, the Consul, she enters the Gentleman's apartment and, like the ashes of *The Burned House,* discovers objects (untouched by the Gentleman in ten years) that bring back memories to her: a clock that was "never right," figurines she treasured, and, oddly, a thermometer, which she refers to as "a family symbol—of inconstancy"; she elaborates: "I'd promise to put it out—and I'd forget. . . . He'd promise to put it out—and he'd forget. . . . We'd nag each other about it, and finally, just to get shut of it, I hid it in this drawer. . . . Know what that means? Well, no one believed our marriage would last because we were both unmasked at once and showed each other our antipathies. . . . From the very first we lived as though we were mounted on springs—ready to fly off at a moment's notice."[45] The power of these objects makes her sentimental and wishing for her life to be better; the feeling (coupled with fear of the unknown) impels her to stay and confront the Gentleman, and they hash out their marriage in the ensuing scene. The Gentlemen's quietude is ultimately broken by the crisis over the daughter being in the hands of the lawless stepfather, and ultimately he helps mother and child escape to greener pastures, returning him to a greater peace than he had enjoyed, secure in the knowledge of his child's safety. Aside from the aforementioned "discovery" scene, very little is used onstage; the only other prop of note is a telephone in which news is conveyed; the result is to place a great deal of focus on the scene as a transformative moment for Gerda.

Summary

While Strindberg and Falck experienced setbacks in the project they created, they nonetheless gave birth to a theatre that represented a significant leap forward in the development of modern antirealism, one whose implications wouldn't be fully appreciated until decades later. The effect was undeniable, though; as German expressionistic playwright René Shickele later noted, "August Strindberg is our password."[46] In the dramatic works explicitly designed for the Intima Teater—the so-called Chamber Plays—well-chosen properties are critical to their effectiveness, be they the animus of a ghostly presence or merely symbolic of the past. Harmonic with Strindberg's stated philosophy of focusing on the simple yet powerful, these plays resonate with depth, meaning, and the potential for visual power through the props they call for in the text.

Notes

1. Quoted in Michael Meyer, *Strindberg* (Oxford: Oxford University Press, 1985), 475.

2. Section title quoted in Meyer, *Strindberg,* 483.

3. Olof Lagercrantz, *August Strindberg,* trans. Anselm Hollo (London: Faber and Faber, 1984), 342.

4. Meyer, *Strindberg,* 475.

5. Among the apartment furnishings Strindberg brought to the theatre for use as props were "a palm tree" and "a gilded pedestal" (Lagercrantz, *August Strindberg,* 343).

6. Meyer, *Strindberg,* 496.

7. August Strindberg, *Letters, Vol. II: 1892–1912,* trans. and ed. Michael Robinson (London: Athlone Press, 1992), 768.

8. Ibid., 770.

9. Ibid., 783.

10. Meyer, *Strindberg,* 518.

11. August Strindberg, *The Ghost Sonata,* in *August Strindberg: Selected Plays,* vol. 2, trans. Evert Sprinchorn (Minneapolis: University of Minnesota Press, 1986), 740–42.

12. Ibid., 742.

13. Ibid., 740.

14. Ibid., 741.

15. Ibid., 742.

16. Ibid., 748.

17. Ibid., 757.

18. Ibid., 771.

19. Ibid., 747.

20. Ibid., 752.

21. Ibid., 763.

22. Ibid., 759.

23. Ibid., 782.

24. August Strindberg, *The Pelican,* in *August Strindberg: Selected Plays,* vol. 2, trans. Evert Sprinchorn (Minneapolis: University of Minnesota Press, 1986), 803.

25. Ibid., 805.

26. Ibid., 810.

27. Ibid., 812–13.

28. Ibid., 814–15.

29. Ibid., 830.

30. Ibid., 802.

31. Ibid., 818–19.

32. Ibid., 821.

33. Ibid., 823.

34. August Strindberg, *The Burned House,* in *The Chamber Plays,* trans. Evert Sprinchorn et al. (New York: E. P. Dutton., 1962), 98.

35. Ibid., 79–80.

36. Ibid., 80.

37. Strindberg, *Ghost Sonata,* 748.

38. Strindberg, *Burned House,* 62, 83, and 101.

39. Ibid., 77, as one instance.

40. Ibid., 81.

41. Ibid., 82.

42. August Strindberg, *Storm Weather,* in *The Chamber Plays,* trans. Evert Sprinchorn et al. (New York: E. P. Dutton, 1962), 5–6. The original Swedish title, *Oväder,* is rendered as *Storm, Storm Weather,* or *Stormy Weather,* depending on the translator. I prefer the first of the three, and use it in the text of my article above.

43. Ibid., 17–18.

44. Ibid., 19–20.

45. Ibid., 29.

46. Quoted in Michael Patterson, *The Revolution in German Theatre, 1900–1933* (Boston: Routledge and Kegan Paul, 1981), 43–44.

Rattle Away at Your Bin

Women, Community, and Bin Lids in Northern Irish Drama

Eleanor Owicki

In an early scene in Jim Sheridan's 1993 film, *In the Name of the Father*, a group of British soldiers opens fire on scrap-metal collector Gerry Conlon (Daniel Day Lewis) after mistaking him for a sniper from the Irish Republican Army (IRA). As Conlon races through the streets of his Belfast neighborhood in an attempt to escape, a woman mutters "bastards!" under her breath and begins to beat the lid of her rubbish bin (trash can) rhythmically against a wall. A moment later, we see another woman performing the same action, a calm but determined look on her face. Soon, the streets are full of men racing to hide weapons or confront the soldiers while the women of the neighborhood perform this uniform action, grimly beating their bin lids against walls and the ground.[1] Within the context of the movie, it is clear that the women are offering a communal warning, spurring the men to take action to protect the neighborhoods from the British soldiers. We may also surmise that this is a fairly choreographed, common event; the women seem to know exactly what to do, and perform their "duty" calmly. What may be less clear to American audiences, however, is how pervasive this behavior used to be in Catholic Republican communities throughout Northern Ireland. Sheridan did not invent it for the film, nor was it a practice that was isolated to a few small communities. Indeed, it was one of the most common ways for Catholic women to participate actively in the Northern Irish Troubles.

Between the late 1960s and the late 1990s, Northern Ireland was home to a violent conflict between Catholic Republicans and Protestant Loyalists. This period, which has come to be known as "the Troubles," saw the deaths of over 3,500 people. Although the issues at the root of the conflict were complex, they fell into two major categories: whether Northern

Ireland's Protestant government had violated the civil rights of Catholics and whether Northern Ireland should remain part of the United Kingdom or join the Republic of Ireland. Although most combatants during the Troubles were men, women participated in many ways. This article explores the ways that one type of object reflected and shaped Catholic women's experiences of the Troubles.

As the above scene from *In the Name of the Father* suggests, Republican women were asked to participate in the conflict by banging the lids of their rubbish bins on the streets of their neighborhoods to raise an alarm when police or the British army were conducting raids. This paper interrogates the ways that the circumstances of the Troubles imbued these everyday objects with both sectarian and gendered meaning. This nonstandard use of household objects offered women ways to engage in the conflict while avoiding confrontation and retaining at least the appearance of their traditional roles as protectors of the hearth. In many ways, bin lids then became an iconic symbol for the "proper" roles and duties of Catholic women. After establishing the semiotic significance of the bin lid, the essay examines the ways that Marie Jones and the Charabanc theatre company use an onstage bin lid to highlight and subvert these meanings in their 1987 play, *Somewhere over the Balcony.* Charabanc, which was active from 1983 to 1995, was founded in order to stage the experiences of women in Northern Ireland. From the play's first moments, the women use the associations that surround the bin lid to find spaces of freedom from their assigned roles as wives and mothers.

The Catholic communities in both the Republic of Ireland and Northern Ireland have historically maintained traditional gender roles. As Imelda Foley observes, "the traditional role of women has been perceived as mothers and carers, as unseen supporters of fathers and husbands, keepers of hearth and altar."[2] When the Republic of Ireland wrote its constitution in 1937, it explicitly included this sentiment: "The State recognises that by her life within the home, woman gives to the State a support without which the common good cannot be achieved. The State shall, therefore, endeavour to ensure that mothers shall not be obliged by economic necessity to engage in labour to the neglect of their duties in the home."[3] This wording remains intact in the Republic's constitution to this day. Although framed as beneficial to women, this philosophy limits a woman's purpose to that of mother (and by extension wife) and denies her any role in the public sphere. By promising to make it so she does not need to work to support her children, the constitution assumes that there is no other reason that she might wish to work, denying her agency and autonomy. It also specifically defines "the home" as the space she should occupy, rather than imagining ways her role as a mother might be extended to other spheres. This philosophy, like many other parts of the

Republic's constitution, is drawn from Catholic tradition, and the sentiment is also prevalent within Catholic families in Northern Ireland.

Given this rhetoric, it is not surprising that the participation of women within paramilitary organizations like the IRA was often contested. Women were admitted into the IRA, but they were unlikely to hold leadership positions. Instead, they would generally act as couriers or in similar auxiliary roles.[4] Most importantly, the IRA continued to stress that the only truly appropriate place for women was in the home. By this logic, the more actively women became involved in the armed conflict, the more they became "unwomanly" deviants. How, then, could the IRA ask Catholic women to participate in the Troubles without pushing them to move outside of their prescribed gender roles? One method they found was through the use of bin lids.

Within the context of the Troubles, the bin lid had two primary uses, both of which reinforced the idea that women should act as guardians of their homes. The first was its intended (and arguably universal) use as part of a system for disposing of trash. In these circumstances, the women used the bin lids to protect their homes from dirt and make them more comfortable. Tom Maguire has noted that, in many Irish plays, "The concerns of mothers for their offspring and/or husband are matched by a struggle to maintain the semblance of domestic order in the face of external pressures that threaten it."[5] Just as the Republic's constitution linked motherhood to the work done within the home, this trope suggests that maintaining a clean home might be a way for a woman to fight for and protect her family. In this context, the bin was a vehicle for literally removing any impurities within the home.

In addition to this traditional use, Republican women also used bin lids as alarm systems for their neighborhoods. In these cases, the women moved into the streets and banged their bin lids on their walls and the ground to warn their neighbors of impending police or army raids. Those who heard the warning would then theoretically have time to hide illegal weapons or make an escape if they were fugitives. The warnings were also designed to expand quickly. As the scene from *In the Name of the Father* shows, any Republican woman who heard her neighbors banging their bins was expected to move to the street in front of her house to join in the clamor. In this way, the alert would spread from the immediate area of the raid, giving a significant head start to any fugitives a few streets away.

The gendered practice of banging bin lids was immortalized in the Republican folk song "The Lid of Me Granny's Bin." After describing the way his grandmother heroically drove off the British army with just her bin lid, the narrator offers advice to all Republican women:

Go home kind friends, and go to bed, sleep as best ye can
But if trouble comes along, get out and lend a hand
To all you fair young ladies, if trouble does begin
Get out into your backyard love and rattle away at your bin.[6]

These lyrics reinforce the tension present in the discourses around the role of Republican women in the Troubles. Ideally, the narrator says they should be at home resting, rather than putting themselves in danger. They should not seek out conflict, but only act if the conflict comes to them. Rather than viewing the banging of bin lids as one of many contributions a Republican woman might make to the Troubles, the song frames the practice as her only option for participation. It is also important to note that the song is written from the point of view of a man, and that he is not speaking about any woman, but rather one defined only through her maternal role. Unlike the male heroes and narrators of Republican ballads like "The Men behind the Wire," "The Patriot Game," and "Joe McDonnell," the granny of this song is not shown to have an understanding of the tensions at the root of the conflict or to have consciously decided to enter it.

The song does contain a few references to the titular grandmother using the bin lid for self-defense, but even these show ambivalence about the relationship between women and violence. The narrator sings:

A soldier came right up the stairs, his riffle in his hand
she kicked him with her button boots and along the hall she ran
Then up and stepped another one, some medals for to win
but all he got right up the gob was the lid of me granny's bin.

There are several important clues within these lines. First, the song explicitly states that the soldier has invaded the granny's home (as distinct from her street or her neighborhood). She does not confront him until he has come "right up the stairs," so her action can be understood as an attempt to protect her home, in true maternal fashion. After this first confrontation, we know that she "ran." Although it is possible that she was running towards the next soldier she would confront, there is nothing in the lyrics that directly suggests this. Indeed, it is the second soldier who steps up, not the granny who goes up to him. The more straightforward assumption, then, is that she is running to get away from the first soldier. Rather than actively seeking to return the violence of the soldiers, she defends herself and her home only as a last resort.

Most importantly, the song relies on the humor of a British soldier being so easily defeated by a woman, particularly one with such an ineffectual weapon. Although the British soldiers seek to control the Catholic residents of Northern Ireland, two of them can't even defend themselves against one old lady with a bin lid. Rather than elevating the women to a position of power and strength, this inversion relies on the shared assumption that women are weak and very little *real* damage could be done with a bin lid. The cheerful melody also asks listeners to approach the song in a relatively lighthearted manner. Whereas the songs about male IRA heroes mentioned above employ slow, dramatic melodies, "The Lid of Me Granny's Bin" is a jaunty air with a repetitive, almost singsong tune. It would be difficult to take any story set to this melody seriously.

As this song suggests, the role created for women by the banging of bin lids might have been less public than it initially appears. In many ways the practice only rhetorically expanded the area of the home to include the street immediately in front of the house. The practice required women to leave their homes and put themselves in a potentially confrontational position with the police. At the same time, it was only invoked when the physical space of the home was threatened (as we saw in the song above). The practice could be understood as communal, since women throughout the neighborhood created the alarm together, but it did not ask women to move out of the immediate spaces of their home to initiate contact with each other or the police. As a result, the practice did little to break down the metaphorical barriers that kept each woman confined to and concerned about her own home.

A related process can be seen in the experience of Anne, a Republican woman Begoña Aretxaga profiles in her ethnographic study *Shattering Silence*. Anne was moving guns from one home to another when she encountered a British soldier. Rather than attempting to avoid him or abandoning her mission, she approached and expressed her sympathy for him, standing "all day outside without a cup of tea." This domestic remark immediately put him at ease, and he did not question her when she said she was only running some errands. According to Aretxaga, Anne's gambit is successful because of "the assumption that inasmuch as women do not belong to the public arena, when they walk the streets they are not really there. . . . [B]y virtue of their presence, the streets cease to be a battleground that must be controlled and become an interstitial space linking domestic arenas."[7] The British soldier Anne encountered shared the IRA assumptions both that the only appropriate place for a woman was in her home and that her maternal role made her unsuited for violence. In this case, as with the use of bin lids, a woman's ability to transform any space into a domestic one was a double-edged sword. It gave the women the opportunity to use their gender subversively in order to both take a part in the conflict and avoid arrest. Anne was able to deliver her weapons without detection, and it was rare for women to be arrested for banging the bin lids. Presumably, men would have had a more difficult time evading arrest during these operations. At the same time, this subversion offered little potential for opening up new ways for women to engage in the conflict, if they so desired. This "ruse" would be successful only so long as the domestic role of women remained unquestioned by men on both sides of the conflict.

The Charabanc theatre company interrogates these discourses surrounding bin lids in their 1987 play, *Somewhere over the Balcony.* The play follows an increasingly ridiculous day in the lives of three working-class Catholic women in Belfast's Divis flats. The three neighbors are the only onstage characters, but the audience gets a glimpse of life in their bustling neighborhood as the women narrate and comment on everything they see. From its first moments, the play subverts the meaning of the iconic bin lid. As the play opens, Kate Tidy delivers a monologue to the audience in which she sings the praises of her bin: "See this bin . . . thank God for it . . . Oh, the peace and quiet. If it wasn't for me having my own bin I wouldn't know peace and quiet. They used to laugh at me in these flats . . . 'Look at Kate Tidy with a bin . . . we have rubbish chutes, nobody needs bins in here.' But I was one step ahead of them. I get up at five o'clock every morning when there is not a sinner about and I carry my bin out til my heart's content."[8] An audience member could be forgiven for initially assuming that Kate "thank[s] God" for her bin because it could be used in one of the traditional ways outlined earlier: either as part of an alarm mechanism or to keep her home clean. This is how Megan Sullivan reads it. In *Women in Northern Ireland: Cultural Studies and Material Conditions,* she argues that "the fact that Kate is initially staged with her bin suggests that she is constructed by its political significance and her relation to the state through it. She is one of the deviant women who subverted the state by signaling men of the approaching danger and she is still defined by this action." For Sullivan, the presence of the bin lid rigidly defines Kate as a dutiful Republican woman. Sullivan goes on to argue that "Although women here are obviously constructed through state intervention, they also resist and reverse such intervention" at other points in the play.[9] Although I agree with her assessment of the initial impact of Kate's bin, her reading overlooks the ways that Kate actively uses the prop to resist this overly determined role.

The rest of Kate's monologue immediately counters the audience's initial assumptions about why she "thank[s] God" for her bin. Kate actually values her bin because the act of emptying it gives her the opportunity for a rare moment of peace and quiet. It is her excuse to leave her children, if only for a moment, and to have time alone. Just like Aretxaga's Republican Anne, who in effect enlarged the domestic sphere in order to transport weapons, Kate exploits the assumptions of domesticity that surround the bin. The act of carrying the bin downstairs provides Kate with an excuse for a momentary escape from her home without having her openly challenge the rigidity of the roles that have been assigned her by her gender. By taking the bin with her as she leaves, she converts the area immediately outside her flat into a domestic space and thereby asserts her right to be there. The immediate effects of this transformation are positive for Kate, who gets her peace and quiet, but it does not challenge the notion (shared by Anne's soldier) that a woman shouldn't leave her home except on domestic business.

Later, the play also highlights and subverts the bin lid's potential as an alarm device. A German tourist (who remains unseen and unheard like all the male characters in the play) approaches Kate and tries to buy it. She replies, "Ten pounds? For my bin lid? Away and feel your head. That was the first bin lid ever banged on internment morning . . . [it] was handed down from my granny. It is a collector's item." Her friends Ceely and Rose then tell her that she should charge two hundred pounds for it, and she readily agrees that this would be a fair price.[10] Given that this is the first we have heard of the bin lid's alleged history, it seems fair to assume that Kate is making it up to drive a steeper price for a souvenir of the Troubles. Kate again subverts the iconicity of the bin lid, playing on the tourist's naive belief that he can understand the Troubles by owning a piece of them. The play presents a cynical view of "Troubles tourism," wherein political activists from across the globe descend on Northern Ireland in solidarity with the oppressed Catholics, and expect the Catholic women to feed them and find them places to stay.

On one hand, the deal, were it to come through, would benefit Kate: she would gain two hundred pounds and lose a bin lid that is not worth very much (even if she feels some affection for it). Given the poverty of everyone who lives in the Divis flats, this money would certainly be useful to Kate and her family. At the same time, by choosing not to challenge the tourist's assumptions that bin lids are emblematic of Northern Catholic femininity, Kate in many ways reinforces them. By claiming that the bin formerly belonged to her grandmother, she not only invokes the song "The Lid of Me Granny's Bin," but also further entrenches the notion that the bin lid is a feminine object. When she positions it as an heirloom, she suggests to the tourist that it is so central and important to the role of women in Northern Ireland that it is treasured and passed from mother to daughter. By not challenging the tourist, Kate rejects an opportunity to show him the distance between the image of Republican femininity the IRA presents and the real experiences of Republican women.

Later in the play, the bin lid moves even further from its traditional uses. Believing that an army raid is imminent, the women begin to arm themselves with police raid helmets and truncheons Ceely collected from the streets. The finishing touch to this armory is the bin lid, which is to be used as a shield. In this moment, it has largely ceased to be a bin lid at all. Andrew Sofer's writing on the metaphorical and symbolic uses of props provides insight into how the bin lid functions here. In describing props that are not used in traditional ways, he argues that "Dissonant props . . . thrust their own material strangeness at the audience."[11] While the audience has already become familiar with the bin lid operating in its two traditional functions, they are now confronted with a bin lid entirely removed from its usual circumstances. The fact that the bin-as-shield is placed alongside an actual helmet and the truncheon further highlights the dissonant nature of this prop.

One might read this scene as a moment in which the symbolism of the bin lid as a marker of Republican femininity is exploded rather than merely subverted. The context of the scene undercuts this interpretation, however. First, the play is ambiguous about whether the women intend to use the armor or give it to their husbands. Although they brandish the bin lids and wear the helmets themselves, their dialog suggests that the male characters will be the ultimate recipients of these objects. When Kate offers her friend Rose the bin lid, it is with the comment that "your Tucker is gonna need protection." The semiotic significance of the bin lids that has been established in this paper depends on their being handled by women. To place them in the hands of men (or even to simply suggest doing this) may disrupt the symbolism of the bin lid, but this disruption will not then transfer to the assumptions about women's roles the object is tied to. Further, when a soldier confronts Rose about her "offensive weapon[s]," she immediately informs him that she is polishing them for her husband. "[O]h, you mean *this* is an offensive weapon? (*Indicating the truncheon.*) . . . No it's not . . . well, I suppose it would be if you were to be offensive with it, but it's not goin' to offend nobody . . . it's just for my man's work, and this is only an oul' bin lid I brought out to polish . . . for I'm sure you know yourself how dirty your bin can get."[12] In this moment, Rose calls on traditional female duties in order to defend her actions. First, she argues that she is helping to prepare her husband for work. Thus, the presence of the truncheon in her hand is only temporary; it will soon return to the male hands that would be able to make use of it. Second, she invokes the trope that Maguire describes, wherein the wife keeps her home clean in order to protect her family. When she claims to be polishing the bin lid, Rose presents herself as inoffensive and apolitical. She projects the image of a woman who is more concerned with the cleanliness of an object associated with garbage than with the politics of the Troubles. Just like Anne with her cup of tea, Rose uses the idea of domesticity to transform potentially transgressive activities into socially sanctioned behavior.

Understanding the intended audience for the play also helps to emphasize its critiques. Charabanc was founded in 1983 by five out-of-work actresses who were frustrated by the scarcity of roles for women and the lack of depth in the few roles that were available. They formed the company both to provide themselves with work and to place the stories of Northern Irish women onstage. For their first play, *Lay Up Your Ends,* Charabanc interviewed women who had worked in Belfast's linen mills in the early twentieth century. The play depicts the 1911 strike in which thousands of women walked out of their work at the mill to protest their poor working conditions.[13] The play presents the women as intelligent and politically aware and highlights the ways that the structures of Northern Irish society and industry have failed them. Over the next few years, Charabanc continued this tradition of interviewing Northern Irish women and using their stories to inspire fictional plays. They also wanted to speak to their own working-class communities, who were rarely addressed by theatre. To reach these audiences, they would perform their plays in community centers on both sides of the sectarian divide as well as in traditional theatre spaces. As a result, the intended audiences of *Somewhere over the Balcony* would be intimately aware of both the nature of the conflict and the material concerns that faced the characters as working-class women.

Somewhere over the Balcony is fairly rare in that it uses a bin lid as an onstage prop. It is far more common for Northern Irish plays set in Republican communities to use only the sound of the bin lids. Even plays that seek to highlight the struggles of Republican women tend to use the bin lids only to create the soundscape of a Republican community. Anne Devlin's 1985 play, *Ourselves Alone,* for example, uses the sound of bin lids to punctuate a tense scene in which Donna, the wife of an IRA man, is interrogated by soldiers searching for her husband, Liam. When Donna refuses to give the soldiers any information, they taunt her by suggesting that Liam might be at his mistress Eileen's house.

The first warning that the army is conducting a raid is not the banging of the bin lids, but rather "the sound of Landrovers screeching to a halt and doors slamming, followed by heavily shod feet running."[14] For both Donna and the audience, the sounds of the bin lids come too late to serve their primary purpose as warnings. Instead, the sounds begin as the soldiers describe Eileen's beauty. In this moment, the audience is focused on Donna's emotional turmoil rather than on the political implications of the conflict or army raids. The banging bin lids, the soldiers' taunts, and the cries of Donna's baby work together to create a sensory overload for the audience. Thus, the discordant sound of the bin lids serves more to increase the audience's sympathy with Donna's emotional upheaval than to point to the larger communal implications of this particular raid. In plays that use the bin lids like this, the sound becomes alienated both from the physical objects of the bin lids and from the specific women using them. The audience does not care about the larger situation in Northern Ireland, but rather about the painful situation in which men's callousness has placed Donna. Where the sound of bin lids comes from is largely irrelevant.

By bringing the actual bin lids back onstage, however, *Somewhere over the Balcony* rejects this abstraction. Unlike *Ourselves Alone,* it does not invoke the vague idea of a Republican woman who, only concerned with the preservation of her home, dutifully bangs away with her bin lid. Instead, both the women and the bin lids are physically present. The play does not demand a realistic set, so in most productions props like the bin lids would be among the most realistic elements of the design. Presumably, the bin lid would be tarnished and dented, showing the history of its use. It would be an actual bin lid, rather than the abstracted idea of a bin lid that appears in plays like *Ourselves Alone.* This is particularly significant given that most of the characters referenced in the play never appear onstage themselves. In Kate's transaction with the German tourist, for example, the bin lid is more tangible than the man who is attempting to purchase it. Rather than transforming the women who use bin lids into offstage abstractions, the play reserves this treatment for everyone else. Although Kate, Ceely, and Rose may share some concerns with the iconic Republican woman, the play refuses to let the audience become comfortable with this stereotype.

As this article has argued, bin lids were highly symbolic within the context of the Northern Irish Troubles. They offered multiple ways for women to fulfill their traditional duties of protecting their home and family, while also identifying the women using them as members of the Republican community. The pervasiveness of this trope, however, allowed Marie Jones and Charabanc to use these everyday objects as sites of resistance. The women of *Somewhere over the Balcony* spend the play navigating the roles that have been created for them by their gender and religion. Rather than openly challenging these constructions, they take pleasure in the little moments when they can subvert them. Many of these moments take place around bin lids, because they immediately signal ideas of "womanliness" and "Republicanness" to Northern Irish audiences. Although *Somewhere over the Balcony* by no means provides a blueprint for women to cast off all patriarchal assumptions, it does give the characters the opportunity to subvert their roles in playful, comical ways. It also seeks to denaturalize these assumptions, which may be a first step to moving beyond them.

Notes

1. *In the Name of the Father,* DVD, directed by Jim Sheridan (1993; Universal City, CA: Universal Studios, 1998). My thanks to Kyna Hamill for reminding me of this scene.

2. Imelda Foley, *The Girls in the Big Picture: Gender in Contemporary Ulster Theatre* (Belfast: Blackstaff Press, 2003), 25.

3. "Bunreacht Na Héiarnn/Constitution of Ireland," Department of the Taoiseach, http://www.taoiseach.gov.ie/attached_files/pdf%20files/Constitution%20of%20IrelandNov2004.pdf (accessed April 26, 2009).

4. For a more exhaustive description of the ambivalence around the roles of women within the IRA, see Susanne Greenhalgh, "The Bomb in the Baby Carriage: Women and Terrorism in Contemporary Drama," in *Terrorism and Modern Drama,* ed. Dragan Klaic and John Orr (Edinburgh: Edinburgh University Press, 1990), 163–83.

5. Tom Maguire, *Making Theatre in Northern Ireland: Through and Beyond the Troubles* (Exeter: University of Exeter Press, 2006), 104.

6. Blackthorn, "The Lid of Me Granny's Bin," on *Irish Songs of Freedom,* Arran, CD, 2000.

7. Begoña Aretxaga, *Shattering Silence: Women, Nationalism, and Political Subjectivity in Northern Ireland* (Princeton, NJ: Princeton University Press, 1997), 38, 39.

8. Marie Jones, *Somewhere over the Balcony* (1987), in *Four Plays by the Charabanc Theatre Company: Inventing Women's Work,* ed. Claudia Harris (Gerrards Cross, Buckinghamshire: Colin Smythe, 2006), 183.

9. Megan Sullivan, *Women in Northern Ireland: Cultural Studies and Material Conditions* (Gainesville: University Press of Florida, 1999), 162, 163.

10. Jones, *Somewhere over the Balcony,* 188.

11. Andrew Sofer, *The Stage Life of Props* (Ann Arbor: University of Michigan Press, 2003), 25.

12. Jones, *Somewhere over the Balcony,* 197, 201–2.

13. Martin Lynch and Charabanc Theatre Company, *Lay Up Your Ends,* ed. Richard Palmer (Belfast: Lagan Press, 2008). For a more extensive history of the company, see Foley, *Girls in the Big Picture,* 29–57.

14. Anne Devlin, *Ourselves Alone* (New York: Dramatists Play Service, 1999), 63.

Bearing Witness

The Noose as an Iconic Prop in African American Theatre

Adrienne C. Macki

As a horrific relic of our cultural memory, the lynching noose represents a period of American history that stirs visceral emotions. From 1880 to 1930 (the end of the Reconstruction through the beginning of the Depression), there was widespread support for lynch mobs in the old South among the white establishment. In the late 1930s African American blues singer Billie Holiday popularized the lynching protest song "Strange Fruit." At the same time, a flurry of lynching dramas appeared in response to anti-lynching legislation. Black and white activists, such as African American poet and playwright Georgia Douglas Johnson, submitted lynching plays to the National Association for the Advancement of Colored People (NAACP) to be performed by local branches, encouraging support for the Wagoner-Van Nuys Anti-Lynching Bill. Although many of these plays are now forgotten in archives, they were once stage worthy and incredibly important to local groups, community organizations, and Little Negro Theatre companies. The phenomenon of staging politically subversive dramas concerned with the specter of the lynching noose warrants further analysis to consider the development and significance of the iconic noose as a stage property.

In this essay, I evaluate the increasing representation of the lynching noose in performance, along with its meaning and dramaturgical function as an explosive, iconic, transformational theatrical prop in five representative lynching plays. My work focuses primarily on works by African American playwrights from what I term the second and third wave, or phase, of lynching drama, but also includes a noteworthy example from the first phase. For the sake of clarity, the three categories include: the initial phase from roughly 1858 to 1937, the second phase from 1938 to 1961, and the third phase from 1962 to the present. The first wave of lynching drama, which has received greater scholarly attention, reflects the trend towards stage realism and folk drama but largely restricts the depiction of brutal violence onstage. The second phase often places the lynching onstage and incorporates the noose as a critical, experimental component of its otherwise realistic dramaturgy.[1] Here, the noose serves as a catalyst for dramatic action and/or supplies the play with its havoc-wreaking climax. The third phase, launched by Adrienne Kennedy's *Funnyhouse of a Negro,* tends to invoke departures from realism with stylized, expressionist interpretations of the lynching scene.

While these phases overlap, they offer a model to evaluate the role of the noose dramaturgically. Analysis of the noose onstage is complicated by the fact that the lynching drama genre resists periodization because many early lynching plays have been (and perhaps remain) lost. My research has uncovered several unpublished manuscripts. Each rediscovered text offers a new perspective, expanding on Kathy Perkins and Judith Stephens's seminal anthology, *Strange Fruit: Plays on Lynching by American Women.*[2] Long lost plays add to *Strange Fruit*'s important chronological index of known lynching dramas.

Furthermore, closer scrutiny reveals that the genre of lynching plays (especially those from the middle period) reflect the incendiary presence and/or frequent allusion to a trinity of potent symbols: the lynching mob (as a sign of mass misrule); the trope of a gun (either brandished onstage or confined to a threatening sound effect catapulting the dramatic action); and finally, the most complex and unsettling of all, the noose onstage.

My study is mainly concerned with the depiction of the noose onstage in African American theatre to illustrate how the prop noose functions as an object capable of advancing dramatic action, reflecting and refracting dramatic meaning, and inciting audience reaction by ritually extolling or exhuming the dead. As Andrew Sofer suggests in *The Stage Life of Props,* a prop can also be "fetishized" or "defamiliarized" through its manipulation and placement onstage.[3] This is especially true of the lynching noose.

Although previous studies have effectively highlighted the anti-lynching movement as well as considered the impact of race, gender, and class politics on lynching drama, or focused on the work of one playwright, few have probed the historical role and evolution of specific theatrical devices onstage (besides the act of prayer and song).[4] My work addresses this gap by emphasizing the reinscription of the lynching noose in African American theatre and pays special attention to a period with a dramatic increase in the writing and production of lynching plays by amateur groups, church organizations, social clubs, and Little Negro

Theatres across the country. According to available records, from 1916 to 1936, eighteen lynching plays were written. From 1937 to 1940, a dozen more appeared, demonstrating the mounting concern in the black community surrounding anti-lynching legislation.[5] The prolific period of the 1920s through the late 1930s (the later part of the first wave through the transition into the second wave of lynching drama) and its impact on future generations of black dramatists is of particular interest as I examine the use of the noose in two previously unpublished, unknown plays—"The Lynching Bee" (1924) by Lelia Miller and "Conscience" (1938) by Harriet Robinson—as well as evaluate how the noose is radically reappropriated in Langston Hughes's *Don't You Want to Be Free* (1938), Adrienne Kennedy's *Funnyhouse of a Negro* (1962), and Suzan-Lori Parks's *The Death of the Last Black Man in the Whole Entire World* (1989).

The following analysis extends Trudier Harris's observation that the "centralized treatment of lynching and burning scenes [in literature] grew in inverse proportion to the number of Blacks lynched and burned historically, but in direct proportion to the cruelty with which such acts were carried out and to the increased political significance they served."[6] Though there were fewer incidents of mob violence in the late 1930s, there was a discernible rise in lynching dramas between 1937 and 1939 as well as increasing political pressure to stop lynching. Plays such as "The Lynching Bee" and "Conscience" spoke to the desire of regional NAACP branches to raise awareness and reform legislation by staging such works in their respective communities. Similarly, plays like *Don't You Want to Be Free, Funnyhouse of a Negro,* and *The Death of the Last Black Man in the Whole Entire World* represented the legacy of lynching on the black community.

This essay also builds on Harvey Young's study of the black lynched body, which reads the fallen figure as "the souvenir, the fetish and the performance remain."[7] I contend that the noose onstage is a souvenir of America's sordid history of racism and violence and "renders visible" the lynched body and the act.[8] In this way, the noose not only bears witness to America's preoccupation with "rough justice," but also conjures the volatile mob's collective embodiment as well as the carnivalesque aftermath where crowds gathered jubilantly, dressed in their finest attire and equipped with picnic baskets, sticks, and rifles.[9] Mothers, fathers, and children participated, often clamoring for relics of the lynched body.

Phase One: Absence of Onstage Violence in Lynching Plays

The lynching plays from the first wave (before 1937) include the works of such African American women playwrights as Angelina Grimké, Georgia

Douglas Johnson, May Miller, and Mary Powell Burrill. Works in this early phase are distinguished by a palpable absence of the actual noose as a prop onstage—and ultimately the absence of enacted violence onstage.[10] Instead, the lynching is either narrowly avoided or the execution and its effects on the community are described in excruciating detail. Plays from the first wave, such as Johnson's *Blue-Eyed Black Boy* or *A Bill to Be Passed,* tend to represent the victim's family and/or community praying for intervention, consoling each other, or struggling with the aftermath of racial violence. Within this construct, one character functions as a messenger as in classical Greek tragedies, relaying the gruesome acts occurring immediately off stage. Alternately, as exemplified by Grimké's *Rachel* and Johnson's *Safe,* works from the first phase illustrate how black mothers escaped lynching by sacrificing their own lives and/or those of their children.

It is telling that many lynching plays from phase one avoid showing the lynching noose and spectacle of mob violence. A simple explanation for this might be that playwrights wrestled with competing mandates to uplift the race and restore dignity and truth while combating concerns that illusory representations of lynching were distasteful, indelicate, grotesque, or even dangerously subversive. Worse, would placing the noose onstage inadvertently elicit the same sadistic pleasure that fueled white power movements? Regardless, the noose's absence reveals the provocative and controversial nature of lynching. The mere appearance of the noose had the potential to inflict the pain that accompanied the actual act of violence; such violence was entirely too common in the early 1910s and 1920s. During this period, as Herbert Shapiro points out, "all blacks lived with the reality that no black individual was completely safe from lynching."[11]

The most notable exception in the first wave is a recently recovered play, "The Lynching Bee," written in 1924 by Lelia Miller. This little-known play, rediscovered by the author in the archival records of the NAACP, bravely dramatizes the lynching event, incorporating the mob's frenzied and irrational formation onstage. It is significant that, unlike the more "genteel" Georgia Douglas Johnson, Miller explicitly blames white society for using black men as scapegoats.[12] "The Lynching Bee" is also unique in that it is one of the earliest plays to deliberately place the lynching attack onstage. The stage directions explicitly describe how the principal character, Snowden, is "dragged roughly" with a "rope around his neck."[13] The prop noose not only conveys his oppressed state, but also advances the dramatic action and holds phenomenological and semiotic significance. As Bert States explains, the "actor takes us into a world within the world itself. At bottom, it is not a matter of the illusory, the mimetic, or the representational, but of a certain kind of actual."[14] Snowden's noose is symbolic and actual; it restrains him and foretells of the imminent danger even as he stands his ground, valiantly protesting. When the restrained victim assails his attackers for their hypocrisy and senseless vengeance, he declares, "I know you all goine ter kill me anyway so I might as [well] say jes what I think. De day will come when all culled people stan together den dere aint goine tere be no lynching."[15] Considering the play's "materialist semiotics," its concern with the "social and cultural work produced and performed . . . in negotiation with their local audiences in particular cultural and theatrical settings and contexts," as Ric Knowles proposes, provides a way to read Miller's dominant image of the noose as a rallying call to black readers and audiences.[16]

"The Lynching Bee" insists that anti-lynching crusades must be fought literally with physical might and militia; such brutal acts require national intervention. The play's conclusion, with a troop of black federal soldiers halting the lynching bee, represents a stalwart desire for increased regulatory control and announces the need for black collective power. This radical, revolutionary scene turns adversity into triumph and illustrates how the lynching noose functions in this play as a tragic reminder of democracy's instability or impossibility in a nation governed by mob rule and extralegal justice. Miller's direct representation of lynching may have been too subversive in the early 1920s. For this reason, it may never have been staged during the playwright's lifetime.

Phase Two: The Noose Takes Center Stage

Whereas "The Lynching Bee" advocates for governmental oversight, Harriet Robinson's short one-act play, "Conscience," proposes that increased education would raise consciousness and effectively stop lynching. This recently recovered text from the second wave of lynching dramas was performed by the Youth Council of the Detroit branch of the NAACP in 1938. In it, a conflicted white boy, Clem, is wracked with guilt after participating in a lynching bee. As if in a nightmare, the cacophony of the mob's incessant, roaring chants and the victim's pleas for mercy haunt him.

One of the dramatist's most provocative scenes involves a stylistic representation of the lynching. Robinson's *silhouetted* figure of a hanging man juxtaposed by an African American servant singing "Nobody Knows the Trouble I've Seen" contributes to her almost Brechtian dramaturgy. As in Charles Dickens's *A Christmas Carol,* the "ghost of horrors past" (in the figure of the lynched character) visits the boy and effectively appeals to the boy's conscience. As a result, the noose in "Conscience" points to the victim's humanity in contradistinction to the mob's barbarity and the nation's pervasive, widespread ambivalence. While the playwright takes the nation to task for its inertia, she maintains that legislative discourse is not the solution; greater systemic changes are necessary. According to her preface, further education and outreach would instill "greater human understanding."[17]

While "Conscience" reflects the lynching rope as a critical component of its dramaturgy, its impact on the genre is not nearly as profound as acclaimed author Langston Hughes's widely performed *Don't You Want to Be Free*. This highly stylized, episodic protest play premiered at Hughes's Harlem Suitcase Theatre in 1938 and not only adds a new dimension to the depiction of the noose onstage, but also is an important precursor to the Civil Rights movement.[18] By December 1938, the show had been viewed by almost ten thousand spectators.[19] Unlike most noncommercial productions, it enjoyed a record run, with 135 performances in Harlem, playing to "students, teachers, artists, members of labor unions, tourist groups, members of college sororities, and church groups."[20]

The stage properties play a fundamental role in the production's concept and company's aesthetic goals. At its opening, director Hillary Philips remarked, "If your props tell a story, you don't need scenery."[21] The inclusion of specific stage properties—a noose, a whip, and an auction block—form "an integral part of the action," and serve as deliberate iconic referents announcing Hughes's political agenda.[22] These props help identify the characters as allegorical figures enduring the collective trials of blacks in the United States. Moreover, Hughes's carefully selected props do not strive for "an illusion of a milieu," but instead, as States and Roland Barthes suggest, attempt to "'infiltrate a question' into the security of stage illusion and, by extension, into the passive security of the audience."[23]

In fact, the sanctity of stage illusion is purposely upended in *Don't You Want to Be Free*. After touring Moscow's theatres, Hughes envisioned a people's theatre in Harlem incorporating modern Russian staging techniques and stories relevant to African American audiences.[24] The principal design of the platform stage signifies an African tom-tom, which underscores the playwright's interest in African ritual. This innovative arena-style staging contributes to a distinct, postcolonial scenography that incorporates Brechtian dramaturgy with a hybrid of African and constructivist imagery fusing Russian staging techniques with historic symbols of racial violence and oppression in America.

Hughes consciously utilizes the lynching noose in a particularly rich and evocative manner, as demonstrated in the following stage directions from an early draft manuscript: "[The play] should be presented in a modern manner with no curtains or stage effects other than a lynch rope which hangs at the back, center, throughout the entire performance, and serves as a symbol of Negro oppression. This rope is used actively only in the lynching scene when the Young Man puts his head into the noose on the words, 'All you cracks got me.' He takes his head from the noose on the words, 'Not I.' Symbolic of the eternal resurrection of an oppressed people."[25] In performance, the noose's constant presence and the young man's interaction with it emphasizes not merely one specific lynching event, but rather an epic history of mob violence as well as Hughes's desire to mobilize audiences against such atrocities. Read phenomenologically, Hughes juxtaposes the horror of lynching with the potential to endure.[26] Whether or not his intentions achieved the desired result is unclear. The *New York Amsterdam News,* a local black periodical, observed that the young Earl Jones's (father of James Earl Jones) performance in the lynching scene "outwardly stirred" the audience in Harlem, suggesting the chilling effect of the onstage noose.[27] A reviewer from the play's L.A. run in 1939 noted in the Communist periodical *People's World* that "the play is sometimes too extreme, too violent, too crude."[28] It is possible that audiences missed Hughes's message of faith and perseverance in his dramatization of the noose.

The lynching scene in *Don't You Want to Be Free,* unlike in "Conscience," does not deliver a cathartic, tragic climax; instead, it deliberately disrupts the traditional narrative by pointing to multiple stories of lynching and sorrow. Indeed, this is reinforced by the noose's continual presence onstage as well as its strategic placement, hanging above center stage between two semicircular platforms, as indicated in figure 2. This enduring reminder serves as a constant tension and commentary on the pervasive threat of lynching in the United States. This effect was not lost on the critics, as suggested by Richard Rovere's review in *New Masses,* a Communist periodical: "Every symbol the Negroes have known in those three hundred years was brought into the play—the African tom-tom, the slave block, the overseer's lash, and the lynch rope—all of these and more, with episodes built around them, comments on their significance in the culture of an exploited race."[29]

While the prop's relentless presence functions as a gruesome souvenir of the black experience, the way in which it is used also reflects and refracts the collective history of blacks in America. Rather than realistically imitating the grotesque effect of lynching, the actor engages with the prop in such a way that attempts to distance the character emotionally and intellectually from the act of violence. It is especially significant that the young man defiantly removes the lynching rope from

Scene from *Don't You Want to be Free*. Courtesy of Langston Hughes Papers, James Weldon Johnson Collection, Yale Collection of American Literature, Beinecke Rare Book and Manuscript Library.

his neck and returns to the play's action. Here, he simultaneously represents a legacy of racial violence, but also the possibility of resistance, survival, and hope. Accordingly, Hughes's progressive, transformative scene also fundamentally departs from traditional lynching narratives. For example, whereas the victim in "Conscience" is limited to a ghostlike presence, the victim in *Don't You Want to Be Free* "survives" and his removal of the noose "signifies" on the lynching trauma.[30] Hughes offers, as David Krasner puts it, a "performative subversion of white authority, undermining and destabilizing racist stereotypes."[31] This strategy of resistance, "signifyin'," functions as a rhetorical device or system of codes that deconstructs white language (or in this case objects), according to Henry Louis Gates. This reclamation and revision of the noose helps pave the way for artists like Adrienne Kennedy and Suzan-Lori Parks, whose efforts further modify the lynching mise-en-scène.

Phase Three: Fetishizing and Defamiliarizing the Noose

What Hughes was to the Harlem Renaissance, Kennedy is to contemporary African American playwrights. As "one of the most influential avant-garde playwrights of the twentieth century," Kennedy launched a "revolutionary style in African American theatre."[32] Her surrealistic plays often traverse subconscious terrains and "freely play with the historical" records as well.[33] In *Funnyhouse of a Negro,* Sarah, the young biracial student, wrestles with her warring identities. Her fractured selves succumb to the pressures of hegemonic society and cause her to loath her blackness.

Though the play affirms a troubling preoccupation with hanging and death, few scholars, other than Philip Kolin, have discussed the enigmatic noose in *Funnyhouse*. Kennedy's radical redefinition of the role of the noose, through repetition, revision, and fetishization, opens up the play for new modes of inquiry. The noose's recurrent appearances foreshadow Sarah's troubling demise while its varied transformative states (of rest and action) simultaneously revise and fetishize the prop. Sarah bears the hangman's rope around her neck in her initial entrance. The significance of this curious tableau is brought into relief when Sarah's landlady reveals that the young woman's father has (allegedly) hanged himself. According to the stage directions, "a bald head is dropped on a wire" and on a "string," which provides two conspicuous visuals of the noose in action.[34] These startling moments flank Sarah's long monologue in which she specifically refers to her father's hanging. Later, another character, Duchess, who is in fact one of Sarah's selves, is discovered hanging from a chandelier. Finally, one of the last images of the play is of Sarah hanging, which begs the question: has she committed suicide or has she been lynched by one of her white selves?

While few scholars have focused on the noose, several have grappled with whether or not Sarah's death is suicide or murder. E. Barnsley Brown maintains that it "is best read as the death of her Negro self(ves)."[35] Tanya Augsburg proposes that the "frightful image of the hanging Negro could be an allusion to lynching," which I agree with.[36] Kennedy's uncompromising tone suggests that Sarah's death is not entirely a solitary act—it is a kind of murder aided and abetted by a mob masquerading "as either white, black, or yellow representative leaders of both genders with whom Sarah personally identifies."[37] Observing Sarah's hanging figure, her landlady as well as her boyfriend, Raymond, laugh and curse her as spectators often did at lynching bees. More importantly, the unremitting specter of the defamiliarized, iconic prop reinforces the reading of Sarah's death as a lynching. The biracial woman is castigated for desiring to be white and for taking up with a white Jewish lover, revealing a multi-tier racism in which African Americans are relegated to the bottom. As Kolin argues, the protagonist is "a victim of white history and her own schizophrenic guilt[;] Sarah receives the same punishment allotted to the condemned sexualized black man, the lynching noose."[38]

However, Sarah's murder is complicated by the fact that the ritual of violence has been internalized to some degree. It could be understood that the lynch mob has shifted from a localized, external entity to an interior, subjective one: a host of fragmented personalities that represent Sarah's other identities. On the other hand, her identities are fully realized entities that bear the brunt of institutional racism and turn against Sarah. Moreover, in performance, the surreal projected figures, Jesus, Patrice Lumumba (an assassinated anti-colonialist African leader), the Duchess of Hapsburg, and Queen Victoria, are typically played by individual actors whose corporeal presence is undeniable. These historical characters are joined by other material witnesses as well—the landlady, the mother, and Raymond—who participate in Sarah's dismemberment and death. Reading the stage action as States might, the noose as a prop and the actors as the angry mob provide "a certain kind of actual" contributing to an unsettling approximation of the spectacle of lynching.[39]

Similarly, the various acts of self-flagellation by Sarah's projected selves are distorted carnival images of the mutilation and lynching of black victims. Indeed, the fistfuls of hair and bald heads in Kennedy's hallucinatory dreamscape bear an uncanny resemblance to the collected souvenirs from lynching bees. Likewise, if the fractured selves are viewed phenomenologically as a volatile mob, then the play's climactic scene can be understood as a lyrical revision of the lynching bee, replacing the southern landscape with an urban, nightmarish jungle. Furthermore, according to the stage directions, Sarah's "father's black figure with bludgeoned hands rush upon her," suggesting that his hands subsume rather than save the young woman.[40] His bludgeoned hands are metonymic for the vicious mob lunging for a relic from the carnage. Accordingly, the noose around Sarah's neck is inexplicably linked with lynching, but the ritual of violence is possibly self-inflicted as the tormented woman desires death as the logical outcome of her projected internalization of hegemonic culture. Therefore, the noose and her ensuing death are also metaphorical, representing her suffocation in the wake of assimilation or, in other words, the threat of erasure haunting black culture. Alternately, the noose itself symbolizes the racist, oppressive acts of white society. Brown maintains that "Kennedy's message is unmistakably that ratiocinative white culture kills—not only the black self/soul but also, simultaneously, the other constructed selves."[41] If whiteness and blackness are in lethal opposition to each other in Kennedy's play, then white culture is literally and figuratively actualized in the looming figures surrounding Sarah. Functioning like a lynch mob, they are unmistakably implicated and observe her untimely death.

In performance, Kennedy's stage directions can be fully explored to flesh out this mob mentality and the potent, dangerous lynching noose. For example, in a 2006 revival by the Classical Theatre of Harlem, director Billie Allen (who had originated the role of Sarah) included a rope that descended directly above Sarah's bed (which resembled a large coffin), and all of the characters mobilized to form a savage mob. In an interview, Allen made her intention clear: "all the selves are in her bedroom, circling her, taunting her, forcing her to give up. They want to see her dead. Circling and chanting their discontent, they drive Sarah to the noose, which she gladly accepts and embraces."[42] The whirling, gyrating patterning of their movement mimics the mob mentality. This effect was acknowledged by critic Mark Blankenship who noted that "her various selves circle her bed and mock her blackness," with their jeers escalating into a barely intelligible pandemonium.[43] Clearly, Allen's direction challenges the premise that Sarah's tragic death is a suicide; these figures are embroiled in her demise.

Kennedy's surrealistic effects and use of repetition provide an important model for Suzan-Lori Parks, who is also well known for her avant-garde style. Parks claims repetition and revision, or "rep and rev," as critical components of her work. Such elements are equally embedded in her highly revisionist history play *The Death of the Last Black Man in the Whole Entire World*.[44] As in *Don't You Want to Be Free* and *Funnyhouse,* the act of performance concretizes the noose's multiplicity and engages the lynch rope in an unusual way to respond to racial violence, signify on lynching, and subvert oppressive stereotypes. Parks's onstage witnesses (a community of black stereotypes, literary allusions, and historical figures) reveal that the principal character, Gamble Major, or Black Man with Watermelon, has been executed by several means (such as electrocution, lynching, and drowning), and yet his figure endures. Similarly, as in "Conscience" and *Don't You Want to Be Free,* Black Man with Watermelon remains onstage with the noose literally and figuratively tied to him, placing him in a liminal state of being and not being.

It is fitting that Parks dramatizes the lynching act multiple times and significantly revises it. Black Man's urgent desire to break free of the noose remains constant in each refrain and is taken up by the other characters, forming a collective consciousness. However, her revision of the lynching narrative offers a rewarding, celebratory outcome: Black Man escapes and runs with a broken limb. As a result, this cycle of repetition/revision probes the possibility of resistance and renewal.

As parsed in detail by Harry Elam and Alice Rayner, "Parks uses culturally specific language that celebrates the elasticity, power, and poetry of black dialect in a formalized and original structure—one which offers repetition but does not repeat."[45] Not surprisingly, Parks also invokes culturally specific props that rely on repetition without repeating, namely the noose.[46] Throughout the entire play, Black Man struggles to breathe and frequently emits a choking "Gaw" sound emphasizing the noose's silencing death grip. On one level, the noose is symptomatic of the oppressive conditions facing African Americans as well as the ways that society has tried to erase black identity. On another level, Parks signifies on the noose by subtly conflating the image of the noose with the image of a necktie, suggesting that a noose is as common to a black man as a suit and tie are to a white-collar worker. In this shocking parody, the noose simultaneously emerges as an assimilationist straitjacket.

The multiplicity of the phenomenological readings and the material reality of the noose's choke-hold commingle and collide, which enable the Black Woman to engage with her husband and intervene in the lynching narrative even as she grapples with the trauma of loss. In so doing, the souvenir noose is reclaimed as part of his burial rites. For that reason, it is significant that Parks's characters explicitly acknowledge the "noose that stringed him up."[47] Too many unnecessary deaths went unnoticed; Parks rights/writes this wrong. And, by performing the burial rites, the play ritually mourns and extols the dead. In such a context, her references to the oppressor and instruments of torture are a way of recovering history, disarming the hegemony, and reclaiming power. As Elam and Rayner insist, "Parks's play performs the ritual re-membrance of the death of the last black man."[48]

Lelia Miller, Harriet Robinson, Langston Hughes, Adrienne Kennedy, and Suzan-Lori Parks offer a stage property that bears witness to the historic inequities facing African Americans. The noose onstage reflects repression from the time of slave ships, to post-reconstruction segregation, through racial profiling today. As a souvenir of institutional racism, the lynching noose continues to reverberate in contemporary African American drama, but its place onstage has shifted and evolved from the late 1930s. The stage noose ranges from a potential threat in "The Lynching Bee" to a menacing silhouette in the shocking tableau in "Conscience." The omnipresent noose serving as a Brechtian device in *Don't You Want to Be Free* appreciably prefigures the radical semiotic function of the fetishized noose in Kennedy's *Funnyhouse of a Negro* and in Parks's *The Death of the Last Black Man in the Whole Entire World*. Moreover, in the latter, the noose is rendered unfamiliar by Parks's transformative repetition and revision.

By serving as an evocative reminder of a long trajectory of violence, terror, and oppression, the noose emerges as a powerful symbolic and material prop which is reappropriated onstage, reinscribed, and resurrected for its phenomenological potential. More specifically, the plays in this study illustrate how the noose as a stage property memorializes lynching as an unhealed wound on American national identity. The noose's direct representation onstage in African American theatre demonstrates a highly codified act of resistance and subtle form of protest against hegemonic forces. African American theatre, by means of symbolic, dialogic stage properties such as the lynching noose, delivers complex, bold representations of black resistance and revision and yields potent, discursive results about race and racism, class and power, colonialism, and identity.

Notes

1. This premise builds on Trudier Harris's assertion that "as black writers searched for a distinct tradition and symbolism of their own, lynching and burning scenes reflect stylistic experimentation, symbolic language, and multiple levels of interpretation." Although Harris refers to novels, there is a similar trend in dramatic literature as well. Trudier Harris, *Exorcising Blackness: Historical and Literary Lynching and Burning Rituals* (Bloomington: Indiana University Press, 1984), 71.

2. Kathy A. Perkins and Judith L. Stephens, *Strange Fruit: Plays on Lynching by American Women* (Bloomington: Indiana University Press, 1998).

3. Andrew Sofer, *The Stage Life of Props* (Ann Arbor: University of Michigan Press, 2003), 3, 23, 24, 25.

4. For discussion of song and prayer in lynching dramas, see Judith Stephens, "Racial Violence and Representation: Performance Strategies in Lynching Dramas of the 1920s," *African American Review* 33, no. 4 (Winter 1999): 655–71; and Craig Prentiss, "'Terrible Laughing God': Challenging Divine Justice in African American Antilynching Plays, 1916–1945," *Religion and American Culture: A Journal of Interpretation* 18, no. 2 (Summer 2008): 177–214.

5. The index of lynching dramas in Kathy Perkins and Judith Stephens's *Strange Fruit* accounts for sixteen plays by African American authors. My total excludes two plays by Conrad Seiler as he has been wrongly classified as a black playwright which has since been corrected. See Prentiss, "'Terrible Laughing God,'" 212–13. For the period of 1916 to 1936, I have included two previously unknown plays, "The Lynching Bee," and a theatrical adaptation by Peter Mason of Walter White's *The Fire in the Flint*, which was recently uncovered by Prentiss. I have also discovered evidence of a previously unknown performance, "The Bourbons Got the Blues" and three additional unpublished manuscripts from this later period that can be added to the index, including "Conscience"

by Harriet Robinson, *Place: America* by Thomas Richardson, and "In Darkest Alabama" by Harlan Glazier.

6. Harris, *Exorcising Blackness*, 185.

7. Harvey Young, "The Black Body as Souvenir in American Lynching," *Theatre Journal* 57, no. 4 (December 2005): 640.

8. Ibid.

9. Michael J. Pfeifer, *Rough Justice: Lynching and American Society, 1874–1947* (Urbana: University of Illinois Press, 2004), 2–4, 94.

10. See Barbara B. Lewis, "Public Death: Lynching Drama in the Years of Its Genesis, 1815–1919" (Ph.D. diss., City University of New York, 2000); Koritha Mitchell, "Anti-Lynching Plays: Angelina Weld Grimké, Alice Dunbar-Nelson, and the Evolution of African American Drama," in *Post-Bellum, Pre-Harlem: African American Literature and Culture, 1877–1919,* ed. Barbara McCaskill and Caroline Gebhard (New York: New York University Press, 2006), 210–30; Judith Stephens, "'And Yet They Paused' and 'A Bill to be Passed': Newly Recovered Lynching Dramas by Georgia Douglas Johnson," *African American Review* 33, no. 3 (Autumn 1999): 519–22; Stephens, "Politics and Aesthetics, Race and Gender: Georgia Douglas Johnson's Lynching Dramas and Black Feminist Cultural Performance," *Text and Performance Quarterly* 20, no. 3 (July 2000): 251–67.

11. Herbert Shapiro, *White Violence and Black Response: From Reconstruction to Montgomery* (Amherst: University of Massachusetts Press, 1988), 32.

12. Winona Fletcher, "From Genteel Poet to Revolutionary Playwright: Georgia Douglas Johnson," *Theatre Annual* 40 (1985): 41–64.

13. Lelia Miller, "The Lynching Bee," 12 (copy in Papers of the NAACP, Special Subject File, Group 1, Series C, Box 299, frame 0390, Manuscript Division, Library of Congress [microfilm, University of Massachusetts Library, Black Research Sources, University Publications of America]).

14. Bert O. States, *Great Reckonings in Little Rooms: On the Phenomenology of Theater* (Berkeley: University of California Press, 1985), 46.

15. Miller, "Lynching Bee," 12.

16. Ric Knowles, *Reading the Material Theatre* (New York: Cambridge University Press, 2004), 22.

17. Harriet Robinson, "Conscience," prologue (copy in Papers of the NAACP, Special Subject File, Group 1, Series C, Box 299, frame 0553, Manuscript Division, Library of Congress [microfilm, University of Massachusetts Library, Black Research Sources, University Publications of America]). Robinson forwarded her play to NAACP secretary Walter White in hopes that he would distribute it to regional NAACP branches and publish it in *Crisis.* However, in a memo dated March 7, 1938, White commented that the play "shows fine spirit but leaves much to be desired in the writing action and concept. It's good though that they are thinking of concrete presentations of this sort" (memo from Walter White, Papers of the NAACP, Special Subject File, Group 1, Series C, Box 299, frame 0553, Manuscript Division, Library of Congress). Georgia Douglas Johnson met with similar criticism.

18. For a detailed study of Langston Hughes's Harlem Suitcase Theatre, see

Joseph McLaren, *Langston Hughes: Folk Dramatist in the Protest Tradition, 1921–1943* (Westport, CT: Greenwood Press, 1997), 117–40.

19. George Murphy, "Negro Theatre[;] Harlem Suitcase Theatre," *New Theatre News* (December 1938): 18.

20. Harlem Suitcase Theatre Brochure, Programs and Playbills Collection, Schomburg Center for Research in Black Culture. According to Hughes, it was also performed by educational institutions such as Howard University, Wilberforce University, and Talladega College as well as regional little theatres in Los Angeles, Pittsburgh, Chicago, and New Orleans. Langston Hughes, "A Note on 'Don't You Want to Be Free,'" Langston Hughes Papers, James Weldon Johnson Collection, Yale Collection of American Literature, Beinecke Rare Book and Manuscript Library, Box 292, Folder 4784.

21. Clipping from *New York World Telegram,* June 10, 1938, Langston Hughes Papers, James Weldon Johnson Collection, Yale Collection of American Literature, Beinecke Rare Book and Manuscript Library, Series XVIII Clippings, Folder 13491.

22. Ibid.

23. Barthes quoted in States, *Great Reckonings,* 93.

24. He was especially influenced by Vsevolod Meyerhold's constructivist design and arena staging at Nikolai Okhlopkov's Krasnya Presnya. Hughes remarked in his autobiography how the "entire seating and platform arrangements of the theater were changed, and the whole auditorium was always used as a playing area, front, back and aisles." Russian directors Okhlopkov and Meyerhold engaged Hughes in conversation and invited him to attend rehearsals where he observed how constructivist sets were built. Langston Hughes, *I Wonder as I Wander* (New York: Octagon Books, 1981), 199, 202. Like that of Russian director Okhlopkov, Hughes's experimental vision required an adaptable platform stage that could be used in multiple ways. Gail Lenhoff points out that Okhlopkov's use of platforms owed a debt of gratitude to Meyerhold's "constructivist scaffoldings," and theories of theatre. Gail Lenhoff, "Spectator and Spectacle: The Theatre of Okhlopkov," *Drama Review* 17, no. 1 (March 1973): 92.

25. Hughes, "Production Notes," draft manuscript, "Don't You Want to Be Free," 1, Langston Hughes Papers, James Weldon Johnson Collection, Yale Collection of American Literature, Beinecke Rare Book and Manuscript Library, Box 292, Folder 4781.

26. To facilitate these multiple readings, Hughes recommended inserting a blackout by placing "a small handspot from a flashlight in the first row focused on the face of the dead boy while the Newsboys shout their papers." Hughes, "Production Notes," 1.

27. Marvel Cooke, "Suitcase Theatre Group Is Brilliant in Premiere," *New York Amsterdam News,* April 30, 1939, n.p., Langston Hughes Papers, James Weldon Johnson Collection, Yale Collection of American Literature, Beinecke Rare Book and Manuscript Library, Series XVIII Clippings, Box 563, Folder 13491.

28. Ed Robbin, "'Don't You Want to Be Free' Thrills Audiences of L.A. New Negro Little Theatre Group," *People's World,* April 4, 1939, n.p., Langston Hughes Papers, James Weldon Johnson Collection, Yale Collection of American Litera-

ture, Beinecke Rare Book and Manuscript Library, Series XVIII Clippings, Box 563, Folder 13491.

29. Richard H. Rovere, review of *Don't You Want to Be Free, New Masses,* n.p., n.d., Langston Hughes Papers, James Weldon Johnson Collection, Yale Collection of American Literature, Beinecke Rare Book and Manuscript Library, Series XVIII Clippings, Box 563, Folder 13491.

30. For discussion of signification, see Henry Louis Gates Jr., "Introduction to *The Signifying Monkey,*" in *African American Literary Theory: A Reader,* ed. Winston Napier (New York: New York University Press, 2000), 344.

31. David Krasner, "Parody and Double Consciousness in the Language of Early Black Musical Theatre," *African American Review* 29, no. 2 (Summer 1995): 318.

32. Philip Kolin, "American History/African Nightmare: Adrienne Kennedy and Civil Rights," in *Contemporary African American Women Playwrights: A Casebook,* ed. Philip Kolin (New York: Routledge, 2007), 62.

33. Annemarie Bean, introduction to *A Sourcebook of African-American Performance: Plays, People, Movements* (New York: Routledge, 1999), 4.

34. Adrienne Kennedy, *Funnyhouse of a Negro,* in *Black Theatre USA: Plays by African Americans,* ed. James V. Hatch and Ted Shine (New York: Free Press, 1996), 339, 340.

35. E. Barnsley Brown, "Passed Over: The Tragic Mulatta and (Dis)integration in Adrienne Kennedy's Plays," *African American Review* 35, no. 2 (Summer 2001): 286.

36. Tanya Augsburg, "Genet and Kennedy's Horror Show of Race and Gender," *Theatre Insight* 4, no. 1–2 (Summer 1993): 29.

37. Augsburg, "Genet and Kennedy's Horror Show," 28.

38. Kolin, "American History," 68.

39. States, *Great Reckonings,* 46.

40. Kennedy, *Funnyhouse,* 342.

41. Brown, "Passed Over," 286.

42. Philip Kolin, "Revisiting *Funnyhouse*: An Interview with Billie Allen," *African American Review* 41, no. 1 (Spring 2007): 172–73.

43. Mark Blankenship, "*Funnyhouse of a Negro,*" *Variety,* January 6–February 5, 2006: 64.

44. Suzan-Lori Parks, "Elements of Style," in *The America Play and Other Works* (New York: Theatre Communications Group, 1995), 8–9.

45. Harry Elam and Alice Rayner, "Unfinished Business: Reconfiguring History in Suzan-Lori Parks's 'The Death of the Last Black Man in the Whole Entire World,'" *Theatre Journal* 46, no. 4 (December 1994): 449.

46. See also Alisa Soloman, "Signifying on the Signifyin': The Plays of Suzan-Lori Parks," *Theatre* 21, no. 3 (1990): 73–80.

47. Suzan-Lori Parks, *The Death of the Last Black Man in the Whole Entire World,* in *The America Play and Other Works* (New York: Theatre Communications Group, 1995), 119.

48. Elam and Rayner, "Unfinished Business," 461.

Hawaiian Culture Propped High with Meaning

The Lei Hoaka in Victoria Nalani Kneubuhl's *Emmalehua*

Stefani Overman-Tsai

VICTORIA NALANI KNEUBUHL, a postcolonial playwright of Samoan, Hawaiian, and Caucasian descent, unveils the challenges Hawaiian American women face in their construction of an identity that embraces their heritage, yet still allows comfortable social movement within the dominant U.S. culture present in Hawai'i. Three of Kneubuhl's published plays can easily be categorized as postcolonial. In *Emmalehua* Kneubuhl specifically traces complicated issues of Americanization prevalent in Hawai'i in the 1950s through the negotiation of a specific stage prop, a lei hoaka.[1] Kneubuhl's play is not simply a history lesson of Hawai'i's past. Instead, the playwright weaves history with current struggles native Hawaiians experience with Americanization and the consequences of centuries of colonization. Using traditional and ancient practices, Kneubuhl traces the trials of the protagonist, Emma, and her family as they each struggle to encourage each other not to forget their heritage and give into Americanization. This essay will examine the playwright's use of an ancient lei hoaka and how it highlights the complications for native Hawaiians in a postcolonial society.

Many props are used to signify how characters are reacquainted with their Hawaiian heritage in *Emmalehua*. Many of those props will be discussed in this essay, but it is the lei hoaka that is particularly interesting in a consideration of how postcolonialism is addressed. In the first scene of the play Emma hears the call of Laka, the goddess of hula, after ignoring her grandmother and hula for several years. The call of Laka is transferred from her dreams to her consciousness and the audience by a Greek-like chorus and the lost lei hoaka that Emma finds in her closet.

This specific lei hoaka, a crescent-shaped necklace adorned with human hair and a black boar's tooth, once belonged to Emma's grandmother and holds significant spiritual importance in its association with hula.[2] Once it is brought out in the open, the lei hoaka becomes an active participant in developing the characters of two half-Hawaiian women in the play, Emma and her younger half-sister, Maelyn. The prop passes hands between the two women, revealing their personal views of their heritage, their passion for hula, and their relationship with each other. The development of Emma's and Maelyn's characters via the negotiation for the lei hoaka presents postcolonial issues of reviving lost cultural practices before they are forgotten or buried under the imperialistic changes that come with Americanization. Kneubuhl uses the lei hoaka as a metaphorical and physical example of Emma's rich hula roots, a reminder of her spiritual strength and her responsibility to her family. As a prop, the lei hoaka is able to transcend function and becomes a significant cultural and postcolonial sign.

The power of an object as a sign is what makes props in a play useful as storytelling devices, because a prop can have more visual power as a sign onstage than in ordinary life. In *Great Reckonings in Little Rooms,* Bert O. States asserts that objects become signs when they enter "illusionary space and time."[3] This notion of how objects become representations can lead us to consider objects onstage, such as props, as specific and purposeful plot mechanisms used by the playwright to reveal tidbits of information when language is simply not enough for the descriptive job at hand. Props take on characteristics and reveal important information that the playwright wishes the viewer to recognize. Andrew Sofer's book *The Stage Life of Props* is a useful guide when considering a prop's performative power because an object transcends function when it is placed onstage and "manipulated" by actors.[4] How a prop is manipulated in performance may reveal socioeconomic messages, including cultural practices, identity construction, and the reintegration of heritage into one's everyday life.

The structure of the play *Emmalehua* also manipulates the lei hoaka and raises it above simple decoration. For outsiders to the Hawaiian culture, leis often are reminiscent of island vacation resorts. Rather than seeing a floral necklace placed upon the necks of vacationers, spectators see an artifact made out of human and animal parts. States asserts that art is able to remove an object from a world in which it has become inconspicuous and move it to a stature in which it is seen anew.[5] In this way, Kneubuhl's insertion of this prop into her play plucks it out of a marginalized realm and places it before an audience that will have to see the lei hoaka for its spiritual and cultural significance rather than assume its purpose based on former stereotypes. The lei hoaka in Kneubuhl's play does not sit like a pretty, delicate string of flowers. Instead, it has weight and shape, and its elements signify cultural practices that must be learned and understood in order to receive their due respect. The prop, therefore, becomes a symbol for an almost lost cultural practice that honors an ancient goddess and perpetuates a historical lesson of what is valued or deemed important to this tradition. Because the Americanization of hula has warped most images of traditional dresses, garlands, and instruments into little more than costumes and entertainment, the purpose of wearing particular leis during specific performance traditions is often not appreciated. Traditional hula is a ceremonial ritual that evolved over thousands of generations of oral tradition to express piety and reverence to deities and important rulers. Part of a ritual is the traditional garb and ceremonial adornments that serve in various honorific functions. Kneubuhl breaks through the stereotypical representations of her culture and educates American spectators—Hawaiian or not—about the importance of a past Polynesian custom which relies on important objects, like adornments, in a ritual ceremony.

In order to effectively gain an understanding of the Hawaiian cultural practices presented by Kneubuhl, we need to examine the lei hoaka as a prop for the stage as well as a signifier for the sacredness of hula. By writing a genealogy of semiotics in his first chapter, Sofer thoroughly examines how signs are utilized in storytelling, particularly performance, because a prop does more than "speak" in the theatre; it "perform[s]." Sofer clarifies how props are unique in performance compared to textual analysis because performance and textual sign systems affect the spectator and reader differently. Rather than reading the word for an object and then translating that word into a picture in the mind as one would while reading, a spectator is seeing the object utilized by performers; therefore, the sign or object enters a physical space in a way that is impossible for a literary word. Sofer states: "The prop must mean in the moment, and that meaning is inextricably tied to such contingent circumstances as the physical dimensions of the performance space, the skill level of the individual actors, director, and designers, and the mood and makeup of the audience on a given night. As concrete synecdoches of that dynamic event we call performance, props remind us to keep theatrical meaning at once in our grasp and on the move."[6] As a theatrical prop, then, the specific meaning of Kneubuhl's lei hoaka is that it represents a cultural emblem signifying the importance of retaining one's heritage. The weight of this prop as a sign, however, will affect various audiences differently depending on the production cast, director's choices, and use of design elements. In this manner, the spectator will understand the prop based on the performative elements rather than the textual ones. This is duly important to the lei hoaka in *Emmalehua* because the play is about an ancient performance tradition, hula. Cultural meaning associated with the lei hoaka is transmitted via the play, but the cultural practice discussed is an ancient dance performance in which the lei hoaka serves a ceremonial and ritualized role.

As a prop, the lei hoaka becomes a participant in the action of the play because of its ritual importance and spiritual significance. Sofer addresses how some props are fetishized when they "take on inordinate significance" and become "the focus of a character's desire, fear or anxiety."[7] The foundation for Sofer's ideas about the fetish is influenced by William Pietz's writings.[8] Pietz describes the fetish as the following: "The truth of the fetish resides in its status as a material embodiment; its truth is not that of the idol, for the idol's truth lies in its relation of iconic resemblance to some immaterial model or entity." An object believed to have spiritual power, then, is fetishized by the one adoring it. Furthermore, a prop, like the lei hoaka, is a stage object representing an object with spiritual power. The lei hoaka provokes significant anxiety in Emma, desire in Maelyn, and fear in Kaheka because of its religious power. Hawaiian tradition dictates how one should interact with the lei hoaka when performing the hula. Throughout the play the lei hoaka conveys its fetishized attributes when characters interact with it physically, emotionally, and spiritually. As a tool used for a ritual ceremony to honor a goddess, the lei hoaka symbolizes the act of worship and connects the object to the embodied practice of hula. Pietz explains this process: "[D]esires and beliefs and narrative structures establishing a practice are also fixed (or fixated) by the fetish, whose power is precisely the power to repeat its originating act of forging an identity of articulated relations between certain otherwise heterogenous things."[9] This definition implies that at the birth of a ritualistic practice an object has no immediate connection to a particular practice. Over time, an object is repeatedly used during a ritual or ceremonial practice and therefore becomes a part of its cultural significance. In this manner the lei hoaka became associated with sacred hula and through generations of oral tradition it absorbed the spiritual rules and stipulations traditionally given to the goddess Laka. Therefore, the lei hoaka is powerful specifically for its religious connotations and its role in Emma's family's ceremonial reverence for the goddess of hula. Kneubuhl excellently uncovers these spiritual purposes as fetishes throughout the script, as well as portrays many authentic performative and cultural facets of the lei hoaka and its relationship to hula as a spiritual practice.

If the authenticity of life practices is a phenomenological goal, then signs have to capture spectators in a moment of understanding. A prop used as a sign in a performance medium aligns with States's notion that reality and illusion require a copresence under a phenomenological umbrella. States points out that by watching an illusion onstage we are willing the illusion to become a reality in our imaginations. Therefore, the "sensory effects of theatre" are essential in the transmission of messages from an illusionary platform.[10] Props, costumes, setting, and actors all add substance to the story told from the stage. Props, as objects that are manipulated within the action of a play, heighten the spectators' awareness of nonverbal communication, allowing them to feel as if they are in the real world. As a theatrical sign, the lei hoaka tells a specific story, makes itself a more conspicuous object, and reframes a stereotypical idea of a cultural practice and emblem; all of these are concerns within postcolonial theory.[11]

Emmalehua offers an alternative view of Hawai'i by conveying a traditional embodied practice and how it clashes with Americanized ideals. Setting the play in 1951 as Hawai'i is considered for statehood is a purposeful reminder that Emma's world is conflicted with imperialism and colonialism. Robert J. Young asserts that postcolonialism actively sets out to change the way people think and behave, making people of all color equitable: "Above all, postcolonialism seeks to intervene . . . to produce a more just and equitable relation between the different peoples of the world."[12] By inserting traditional Hawaiian practices, rituals, and struggles into a particular time that is pivotal in American history, Kneubuhl is asking the audience to give equal attention to Hawaiian customs as they are affected by U.S. society. *Emmalehua* conveys many instances of imperialistic rule, which damaged the longevity of ancient cultural practices when western missionaries and businesses colonized the islands. Such drastic imperialistic influences cannot be recuperated from. However, through Emma, Kneubuhl demonstrates that a new path can be charted in which native islanders can learn to embrace their past in the present while they are moving toward a future communal identity as Hawaiian Americans.

Not only is *Emmalehua* an encouraging postcolonial play for the Hawaiian American community, it also exemplifies the current political climate in Hawai'i. There are many activist groups seeking to protect native Hawaiians' rights on the islands as the consequences of colonization have increased instances of poverty, homelessness, and the destruction of Hawai'i's unique environment. To overcome complete western assimilation, Hawaiian activist Haunani-Kay Trask calls for a process of "decolonization" where native Hawaiians resist the influences of Americanization. In her book *From a Native Daughter*, Trask states that the "decolonizing of the mind" is "often mistakenly referred to as 'cultural revival.'" Trask's purposeful use of the term "decolonization" is a political choice to exemplify that a conscious effort to resist "cultural imperialism" is necessary to the future of Hawai'i as an independent entity that assumes a unique identity rather than a warped Americanized notion of Hawaiian identity. Trask asserts: "But decolonization is political at the core because it functions to unscrew the power of the colonizing force by creating a new consciousness very critical of foreign terms, foreign definitions, and foreign solutions."[13] Specifically, decolonization seeks to recognize Americanization as the foreign influence, not the Hawaiian activist's desire for sovereignty and independence. Knuebuhl's play can be described as representing Trask's notion of decolonization through Emma's decision to resist urban development and to reintegrate hula as an authentic cultural practice necessary to her identity as a native Hawaiian woman.

Such a resistance to Americanization is particularly poignant in *Emmalehua* because of the historical moment in which the play is set. The years prior to Hawai'i becoming a state are profound moments in U.S. history, as Hawai'i was the last state to enter into the U.S. union. Politically, this move ensured that the United States had control of the Hawaiian Islands for agricultural and military purposes. Socially, this move opened the doors for many citizens to move from the continental United States to the Islands, further marginalizing the native Hawaiians from their own homeland as urban development enveloped much of the land. Economically, the United States benefited from "owning" Hawai'i and turning it into a profitable tourist industry. Craig Howes, in his introduction to Kneubuhl's island play anthology, points out that the time period of the play is critical to the politics addressed. He notes, "[T]wo aspects of this struggle had a profound impact on Hawai'i's people during the 1950s: a renewed pressure to assume enthusiastically an American identity, and the steady shift towards a tourist economy."[14] This process is exemplified through the character Emma.

The play focuses on Emmalehua—Emma, for short—at the point when she rediscovers a lei hoaka that once belonged to her grandmother, a hula master who taught Emma the sacred art of hula. When her grandmother, Kupuna, died, Emma stopped practicing and performing the hula. After marrying, Emma is further distanced from hula by her husband's desire to participate in pushing the island toward becoming an American paradise. Alika, Emma's husband, is an engineer for vacation resorts, and when one of his projects threatens Emma's family history, she questions her past, present, and future with a man who would bury ancient landmarks for the profits of tourism. At this crucial moment of speculation, Emma is reunited with her grandmother through her dreams and begins to remember the power and importance of hula and her Hawaiian heritage. Ultimately, Emma forsakes Alika's ideals and decides to re-embrace her hula teachings and the memory of her grandmother.

Act I of the play begins with Emma's first disturbing dream, which lingers even after she is awakened by her husband. While Emma searches for Alika's lost tiepin, the Greek-like chorus created by Kneubuhl to enact Emma's dreams draws her to the lei hoaka hidden in the closet. The only interest Alika displays for the lei hoaka is in the human hair strands that may have come from dead people, but Emma's dialogue suggests that she is awed at finding the object. After Alika leaves, Emma falls asleep again and her dream resumes. This time her father, Kaheka, a native man of pure Hawaiian descent, wakes her up. Kaheka takes more interest in the discovery of the lei hoaka than Alika and expresses concern for Emma because she is clutching an object that contains significant mana, or spiritual power. By saying "it came back," Kaheka suggests that the lei hoaka has the power to control its own movement. Kaheka and his mother believed that Emma would be "the one for Laka"; being chosen by the goddess gives Emma a significant amount of cultural and spiritual responsibility to keep the Hawaiian religion and traditions alive.[15] By declaring that she did not want such a legacy, Emma defends her right to ignore hula and her past because being sacred and kapu, the Hawaiian notion of being taboo, was emotionally painful: "You don't know what it was like. You were never kapu (taboo), isolated, alone, so sacred almost no one could touch you. What kind of life is that for a child? . . . Like being an untouchable!"[16] Because the hula style that Emma learned as a child is designed to be performed to honor the goddess Laka, there were stipulations placed upon her as a means to protect her from the spiritual power associated with this particular hula tradition. Hula students studying this type of sacred hula are learning how to respect the sacred power associated with the chants and gestures and therefore must remain separate from others to prevent harming the dancer or others.

While conversing about the newfound lei hoaka in the first scene of the play, Kaheka tells Emma that his mother was going to remove the kapu but died before she could complete the ritual. Kaheka's revelation implies that the lingering kapu may be one reason why Laka is calling Emma back through the lei hoaka: "Five years later, Gramma was going lift the kapu, but all of a sudden, she came real sick. Two weeks later, we buried her. Emma took it pretty hard. (*Pause*) Not good she never lift the kapu. That's why trouble comes to you." Emma dismisses the notion, telling her father that he has a "child's imagination," and refuses to believe that the spiritual strength assigned to her and the lei hoaka is the cause of her disturbing dreams.[17] In act 2, scene 9, Emma admits to her father that she wanted to forget the things her grandmother taught her so that now when she tries, she cannot remember anything: "I wanted to forget so much—everything. . . . And now I can't remember a thing. It's like a fog and I can't see, like big pieces of my life I can't find. . . . Will those things come back?"[18] At this point in the play, Emma actively considers her life without her heritage, hula, and her memories of Kupuna. This moment reinforces the notion that Kneubuhl is dramaturgically using Emma to portray how a person struggles with the emotional consequences of Americanization and begins a mental process of decolonization. By missing her memories and acknowledging that she has a mental and emotional "fog," Emma is regaining control of her thoughts. Her mental "fog" is lifted later in the scene when Emma has a dream that becomes reality. She meets her grandmother in corporeal form and is given an image of Laka, a large lump of wood taken from the trunk of a tree and tied with a piece of yellow kapa, or bark cloth, for which to honor Laka.[19] When Alika and his guests enter their home for a social gathering, Emma is kneeling before the Laka image honoring the goddess. By honoring Laka in such a manner Emma is re-embracing the spiritual connection she once had with the goddess through specific ritualized practices. Not only is this an example of decolonization, but it is also an example of reintegrating a lost embodied practice into one's Americanized society.

Emma's possession of a Laka image complicates her relationship with her husband. Alika is the youngest president of the Association for Engineers and is currently designing a new resort that would cover an ancient fishpond that once belonged to Emma's ancestors.[20] Such destruction makes Emma unhappy, but, in the early scenes of the play, her devotion to Alika makes it difficult for her to stand up against the project. By the end of the play, however, Emma is strengthened by her renewed spiritual connection to Laka and Kupuna, enabling her to stand against Alika's push for Americanizing their home and island. Kneubuhl strategically places Alika at odds with Emma as a way to dramatize the conflicting ideals between those who want to Americanize Hawai'i and those who do not. Such a conflict still permeates Hawai'i's society and is a recognizable argument to native Hawaiians and activists. The desire to remain authentically Hawaiian contrasts greatly with sentiments that the American presence in Hawai'i is economically beneficial, a sentiment brought to fruition for the purposes of Americanization.

Alika is not the only character who provokes Emma to reconsider her heritage as a reliable influence for future choices about how to live as a native Hawaiian in a U.S. society. Another character who clashes with Emma about the importance of the past is her half-sister, Maelyn. Maelyn is Chinese Hawaiian, sharing Emma's father and grandmother.[21] Maelyn was not shown the secrets of the sacred hula by their grandmother. Despite this exclusion, Maelyn became a contemporary hula dancer in Waikīkī and, at the outset of the play, seems to share Alika's dream of Americanizing the Islands.[22] In act 2, scene 2, Maelyn finds the lei hoaka and asks Emma why she didn't tell her about still having it. Maelyn insists that she could use the lei hoaka when she dances in Waikīkī, but Emma insists on putting it away. When Maelyn does not give it up, Emma "aggressively takes it away from Maelyn."[23] The sisters' argument portrays the tension felt between the sisters over hula. Emma was taught hula by Kupuna because she was deemed spiritually special, whereas Maelyn, despite her love of hula dancing, was not deemed special enough to learn the dances for Laka and became resentful toward what she called the "Laka club," Emma and her grandmother. Alone, Maelyn takes the lei hoaka from the closet while the chorus chants that she is not the one Laka wants. But Maelyn fixates her attention on the spiritual emblem; unable to let it go, she steals the lei hoaka when she exits. Later in the play, she returns to Emma's home wearing the emblem and dances seductively for Alika.

This is the same scene in which Alika and his friends find Emma prostrate before the Laka image. Purposely ignoring her sister and the Laka wood, Maelyn takes off her jacket to dance, revealing the lei hoaka. Seeing the spiritual emblem upon Maelyn's neck while she is dancing a touristy hula dance enrages Emma. She pulls the lei hoaka off Maelyn and slaps her face. Alika, embarrassed that his friends see his wife with a native image, gives his wife an ultimatum: "If you don't want to finish things here and now, then get rid of it." By this moment Emma has realized that Alika will never want to have a house and family as she does because his passion is not rooted in family or heritage. Therefore, giving up hula dancing for a man who does not respect her desires is no longer what she wants for her life and future: "I won't erase the past and hand you the future."[24] With this one statement, Emma declares that she is indeed going to reclaim the traditions she ignored upon meeting her husband. It can also be assumed that Emma will now try to stop Alika from ripping up an ancestral fishing pond. Kneubuhl, therefore, exemplifies a woman who bridges her past with her present in order to keep the spiritual beliefs of her heritage alive for future generations. This is the crux of the play and the poignant moment in which Emma regains confidence that her heritage is significantly powerful. What visually drives this message home is the uniting of the lei hoaka with the Laka image. With this unity, the lei hoaka is returned to a place of honor in the presence of the goddess of hula, illuminating the significance of native spiritual piety with iconographic emblems.

The Laka image does not physically remain with Emma, however. In her second appearance in the play Emma's grandmother returns in corporeal form and removes the kapu placed on Emma so that she is free from the restrictions of spiritual sacredness associated with Laka's hula.[25] By doing this Kupuna gives Emma the freedom to choose how and when she dances sacred hula, a notion dramatized when Emma dances with the chorus. In the final scene of the play, Kupuna returns one last time to retrieve the Laka image from Emma. Kupuna takes the image, leaving only the lei hoaka to remind Emma of her spiritual purpose—to keep hula dancing devoted to Laka alive for future generations. Significantly, the section of wood representing the Hawaiian goddess of hula is removed from Emma's life along with Kupuna. Only the lei hoaka remains, which can exist in the ancient times of Hawai'i as well as in its Americanized future, showing a physical transcendence of space and time.

Transmission of ancient stories and practices is an important aspect of oral traditions. As a hula master Emma is free to share her knowledge and has a responsibility to teach hula to other women. After the kapu is lifted from Emma, Maelyn asserts her desire to learn hula and challenges Emma's choice to cast off her spiritual inheritance for a husband. She states, "I would have given anything for what Gramma gave you. I would never have run away from it, especially to Alika." Emma then pledges to teach Maelyn the ancient hula traditions: "When it's time, you'll come to me, and I'll teach you what she taught me. Everything. I promise."[26] It is through this promise that we see Emma's revived desire to practice the sacred dance of her people and her commitment to assume the role of master, which gives Maelyn the privilege of being her first student. As the lights fade to black, Emma, now wearing the lei hoaka, is the only character left on the stage; she is alone on this newfound mission of embracing hula and her heritage so that it will not die in the voids of Americanized forgetfulness.

Clearly, *Emmalehua* is a play that represents the process of reintegrating hula as an embodied practice because Emma must choose to answer the call of Laka or reject it. Kneubuhl's use of the lei hoaka signifies that hula consists of more than flowers and muumuus. As a cultural sign, the prop exemplifies an essence of spiritual power associated with some forms of hula and the importance of proper transmission of hula knowledge from person to person. In her book *Sacred Hula*, ethnomusicologist Amy Stillman addresses various hula styles and the power or sacredness given to them. Stillman makes the point that "not all hula are equal." Specifically, kuahu is a branch of ancient hula that falls under the guidance of Laka. Stillman writes: "The term kuahu refers to altars at which offerings and prayers are addressed to various deities. . . . Within the hula tradition, an altar dedicated to the hula goddess Laka was maintained during the course of instruction. In this sense, a hula kuahu would be a hula whose creation and transmission are bound to the observance of altar rituals honoring Laka."[27] The type of sacred hula that Kneubuhl writes about in *Emmalehua* is hula kuahu, or a very similar type, because the transmission of the sacred hula requires an altar dedicated to Laka, a student, and a hula master.

Kupuna, the master, and Emma, the student, are proven to be connected to the sacred altar twice in the play. The first instance is at the beginning of the play when Kaheka is reminding Emma that she was "the one for Laka." Kaheka states that as a child Emma loved Laka's altar and had a significant effect upon it: "But you loved Laka's altar. . . . You kept everything alive. . . . Everything for weeks, all the flowers, all the ferns and vines, no water, only you. . . . Laka gave you hula. Hula gives life."[28] With this description Kneubuhl exemplifies a symbiotic relationship between goddess and worshipper, Laka and Emma. Laka's altar, despite the belief that the goddess is present, cannot keep the offerings alive without a human conduit. Therefore, Emma's powerful connection to the goddess is necessary for ceremonial and ritual practices.

The second instance in which the altar is referred to is when Kupuna lifts the kapu from Emma. Emma tells Kupuna that she "killed" all of the plants on Laka's altar, and her grandmother comforts her: "Come, come, don't cry. You and I will begin again. Life begins again. . . . Take my hand now."[29] Emma takes Kupuna's hand and they, along with the chorus, build a new altar with live forest greens. Once the altar is complete, Emma and the chorus dance and chant a traditional hula "appealing" to Laka for life. The kapu is lifted, and now that she has a new altar, Emma can practice and teach hula under the guidance of Laka. Now that she remembers the lessons taught to her by Kupuna, Emma is empowered to continue life as a Hawaiian woman rather than an Americanized Hawaiian woman who has forgotten her culture. This is significant because it demonstrates a "decolonized" notion of resisting foreign influence as well as the spiritual significance of Hawaiian traditions.

The dramatization of creating an altar conveys that sacred power is required for one to participate in ritualistic ceremonies like hula. Stillman's examination of hula kuahu can help us understand Emma's defensive actions to protect the lei hoaka throughout the play. Two specific terms that clarify Emma's frustration with her hula past are mana and kapu.[30] Mana means sacred power and signifies the amount of spiritual influence or sacredness associated with an object, person, or action. Kapu, according to Stillman, refers to the "prohibitions that function to protect sacredness by keeping the sacred separate from the profane." Stillman describes the relationship between these two terms: "Mana accrued with rank; the greater the rank, the greater the sacred power. Thus prohibitions were necessary to protect sacred power, and to protect the less sacred from potential dangers of exposure to sacred power."[31] Stillman's explanation of these two terms highlights Emma's reactions when Alika and Maelyn touch the lei hoaka. In these instances, her dialogue and stage directions indicate that Emma does not want Alika or Maelyn to touch the lei hoaka. She hurries to put the lei hoaka away or forcefully removes it from their hands. These performative actions indicate that Emma is aware of the spiritual power associated with the lei hoaka and attempts to follow the strictures of keeping it protected from those without the appropriate amount of mana. When he wakes Emma from her second disturbing dream in the first scene of the play, Kaheka expresses his concern for Emma's well-being. He points to the lei hoaka, calling it "this," and states that it carries a large amount of mana. Kaheka is one of the few characters in the play that respects the lei hoaka's sacred power by not touching it, calling it by name, or reducing its function to that of simple decoration. Instead, he is convinced that the return of the lei hoaka is a significant sign that Emma is being called by Laka and that the predictions about Emma's mana are true.[32] Through these actions Kneubuhl portrays characters of an older generation as respectful of ancient traditions while those of a younger generation are disconnected from the important meanings associated with Hawaiian spirituality and rituals. Emma becomes the link between both generations, amplifying how important it is for her to embrace the traditions she learned from Kapuna.

The lessons taught to Emma by her grandmother were not unusual for those learning hula kuahu. Because there was a lot of mana associated with these hulas, it was important to protect the student as well as those around her from being harmed by spiritual power. Therefore, placing a kapu upon the students would keep them from inadvertently misusing their or Laka's mana. Stillman expresses the complex process a student must endure while in training for hula kuahu: "In the case of hula, the student risked unfortunate repercussions if a piece of repertoire was not learned or performed correctly. A bad performance could also compromise the life force, mana, of the dedicatee. Once students had mastered the repertoire, the lifting of ritual restrictions in graduation ceremonies freed them to perform the repertoire, in full awareness of the multiple dimensions of sacredness they had been entrusted in poetic repertoire."[33] Learning this sacred style of hula creates a bond between dancer and goddess and therefore requires diligent obedience to the restrictions of kupu so as not to diminish one's mana or harm oneself or others unwillingly with their mana. Emma's obedience is exemplified as she takes the lei hoaka from Alika when he tries to touch the human hair that adorns it. Emma also grabs the lei hoaka out of Maelyn's hands when she does not willingly give it up and slaps her when she dares to wear it. It is clear in these exchanges that Emma's actions are still defined by her knowledge that the lei hoaka holds a lot of power and that the strictures of kapu require that she not let someone without the appropriate mana handle it. In this manner, the negotiation of this particular prop presents past cultural practices as active entities in Emma's life. Kneubuhl's use of the lei hoaka clearly depicts a respect for the old ways, but then the entrance of Emma's grandmother and her removal of the kapu equally depict the openness of the future.

In *Emmalehua* the lei hoaka is argued for, argued about, stolen, returned, rejected, and finally embraced. This prop negotiation between the characters perpetuates cultural and familial healing by opening conversations about their shared Hawaiian heritage and the role it has or has not played in their lives thus far in the play as well as reveals a unique postcolonial perspective. Kneubuhl is able to unite ancient traditions with daily struggles in such a manner that the changed, postcolonial present portrays healing characters with the power to keep tradition alive as they venture forward into their currently Americanized island home. Kneubuhl represents Hawaiian heritage through this ancient lei hoaka and reveals how colonialism has deformed a communal understanding of the past, present, and future as the characters interact with this unique prop. The representations that are conveyed in this, as well as other, Kneubuhl plays offer a new perspective on the future of Hawaiian traditions as the island becomes intricately entwined with Americanized practices.

Notes

1. Victoria Nalani Kneubuhl, *Emmalehua,* in *Hawai'i Nei: Island Plays* (Honolulu: University of Hawai'i Press, 2002), 77–141.

2. In an e-mail communication Victoria Kneubuhl described her choice of this particular prop: "When I first wrote the play I was going to make this object a lei niho palaoa (a whale tooth necklace) but decided against that idea because that kind of lei is always a symbol of the alii and a very sacred object. I felt

uncomfortable even making one that was a prop. I decided to use a lei hoaka, a boar tooth necklace because I felt it didn't carry the same heavy cultural weight (and therefore consequences) as a lei niho palaoa, but could still be a sacred object to this particular family because of the mana (spiritual power) imbued in it through the genealogy and generations of this particular family. Cultural objects acquire mana through repeated ritual use" (e-mail communication with author, August 7, 2009).

3. Bert O. States, *Great Reckonings in Little Rooms: On the Phenomenology of Theater* (Berkeley: University of California Press, 1985), 19, 22.

4. Andrew Sofer, *The Stage Life of Props* (Ann Arbor: University of Michigan Press, 2003), 12. Sofer clarifies the difference between "portability" and "manipulation." I agree with his assertion that an object can be manipulated while in a stationary position; therefore, I will also use "manipulate" as the appropriate action-word for the usage of props onstage.

5. States, *Great Reckonings,* 22.

6. Sofer, *Stage Life of Props,* 16.

7. Ibid., 26. I would like to thank Andrew Sofer for pointing out in his closing remarks at the SETC Theatre Symposium that the lei hoaka can be viewed as a fetishized object, as it opened new research avenues to explore.

8. William Pietz wrote three sequential articles, titled "The Problem of the Fetish," on the fetish for the academic journal *Res.* In these articles, published in 1985, 1987, and 1988, Pietz explores how the word "fetish" was misappropriated from its original form. His examination delves into the ritualistic usage of African talismans as fetishized objects. William Pietz, "The Problem of the Fetish, I," *Res* 9 (1985):5–17. William Pietz, "The Problem of the Fetish, II," *Res* 13 (1987):23–45. William Pietz, "The Problem of the Fetish, IIIa," *Res* 16 (1988):105–23.

9. William Pietz, "The Problem of the Fetish, I," *Res* 9 (1985):7–8.

10. Bert O. States, "The Phenomenological Attitude," *Critical Theory and Performance,* ed. Janelle G. Reinelt and Joseph R. Roach (Ann Arbor: University of Michigan Press, 1992), 372.

11. Postcolonialism, as grandfathered by Edward Said in his book *Orientalism,* strives to relocate marginalized knowledge into the dominant academic discussion, an important intersection for cultures that are not adequately represented in dominant academic and political positions. Mark Fortier, in *theory/theatre,* cohesively defines postcolonialism as a means of describing today's world under the consideration of the existence of imperialistic rule in the past (Mark Fortier, *theory/theatre: An Introduction,* 2nd ed. [London: Routledge, 2002], 192).

12. Robert J. C. Young, *Postcolonialism: A Very Short Introduction* (New York: Oxford University Press, 2003), 7.

13. Haunani-Kay Trask, *From a Native Daughter: Colonialism and Sovereignty in Hawai'i,* rev. ed. (1993; repr., Honolulu: University of Hawai'i Press, 1999), 90.

14. Craig Howes, introduction to *Hawai'i Nei: Island Plays,* by Victoria Nalani Kneubuhl (Honolulu: University of Hawai'i Press, 2002), xxi.

15. Kneubuhl, *Emmalehua,* 85–87.

16. Kneubuhl, *Emmalehua,* 87. *Kapu* is defined as "to be prohibited" (Henry

P. Judd, *The Hawaiian Language and Hawaiian-English Dictionary* [Mililani: The Islander Group, 1980], 99).

17. Kneubuhl, *Emmalehua*, 89.

18. Ibid., 129.

19. Ibid., 130.

20. Trask describes this sense of belonging: "Each of the eight inhabited islands was divided into separate districts (known as 'okana), running from the mountains to the sea. Each 'okana was then subdivided into ahupua'a, which themselves ran in wedge-shaped pieces from the mountains to the sea. Each ahupua'a was then fashioned into 'ili, on which resided the 'ohana (extended families), who cultivated the land. The 'ohana was the core economic unit in Hawaiian society" (Trask, *From a Native Daughter*, 4). This explanation clarifies that families lived on certain parts of the islands and were responsible for caring for that portion of land.

21. By creating a character of Chinese Hawaiian descent, Kneubuhl is also acknowledging the extensive Asian Hawaiian population in Hawai'i.

22. Maelyn's career as a dancer in Waikīkī alludes to the misappropriation of hula. Adrienne Kaeppler points out: "[M]uch of the living Hawaiian dance tradition, however, has so radically departed from the traditional that it has become a kind of 'airport art' (tourist attraction)" (Adrienne L. Kaeppler, "Dance and the Interpretation of Pacific Traditional Literature," *Directions in Pacific Traditional Literature: Essays in Honor of Katharine Luomala*, ed. Adrienne L. Kaeppler and H. Arlo Nimmo, *Bishop Museum Special Publication* 62 [Honolulu: Bishop Museum Press, 1976], 201). In this manner, Maelyn is a complicit participant in using hula dancing as a performance model for tourists. It is not until the end of the play that we realize Maelyn wants to learn and observe ancient hula traditions, but she was never taught. Kneubuhl is challenging the Americanized standards of hula that took over the tradition after WWII. Michelle Keown adds that Kneubuhl "contrasts crass appropriations of Hawai'ian hula dancing in the post-war Hawai'ian tourist industry with the specific spiritual and cultural significance of the hula within Indigenous Hawai'ian culture" (Michelle Keown, *Pacific Islands Writing: The Postcolonial Literatures of Aotearoa/New Zealand and Oceania* [Oxford: Oxford University Press, 2007], 216).

23. Kneubuhl, *Emmalehua*, 111.

24. Ibid., 132–34.

25. Ibid., 135–36.

26. Ibid., 137–38.

27. Amy Stillman, *Sacred Hula: The Historical Hula 'Āa'apapa* (Honolulu: Bishop Museum Press, 1998), 23.

28. Kneubuhl, *Emmalehua*, 87–88.

29. Ibid., 135–36. Kneubuhl has written most of this quote in Hawaiian with a parenthetical and italicized translation. Assuming many readers of this article do not read Hawaiian, I have quoted only the English translation as written by the author.

30. Henry P. Judd, *The Hawaiian Language and Hawaiian-English Dictionary* (Mililani: Islander Group, 1980).

31. Stillman, *Sacred Hula,* 23.

32. Kneubuhl, *Emmalehua,* 87.

33. Stillman, *Sacred Hula,* 40. Stillman's quote also clarifies Emma's anxiety about making a mistake while dancing and Kupuna's encouragement for her to begin again.

Revisiting Eva Marie Saint's White Glove

On Props, Neurons, Subtext, and Empathy

Andrew Kimbrough

IN WHAT IS known as the "white glove scene" of Elia Kazan and Budd Schulberg's 1954 film *On the Waterfront*, Eva Marie Saint's good-girl character, Edie Doyle, does not wish to spend time talking in a New Jersey waterfront park with the longshoreman thug Terry Malloy, played by Marlon Brando. As she turns away from him to walk home alone, she takes her gloves from her coat pocket and accidentally drops one. Terry picks it up and, rather than hand it back to Edie, he sits down on a swing, casually cleans the glove of dirt, and then puts it on his left hand. The behavior was not scripted for the film yet it accompanies Schulberg's dialogue, which is mostly uncomfortable small talk initiated by Terry in a labored attempt to seek out a connection with Edie.[1]

For cinephiles the white glove scene has acquired mythic status. It holds a special allure for many reasons, one being that fans of the film appreciate it according to its intended reception. Kazan, providing an authorial, psychoanalytic interpretation of the scene, says, "As they were walking along, she accidentally dropped her glove; and Brando picked up the glove; and by holding it, she couldn't get away—the glove was his way of holding her. Furthermore, whereas he couldn't, because of this tension about her brother being killed, demonstrate any sexual or loving feeling towards her, he could towards the glove. And he put his hand inside the glove . . . so that the glove was both his way of holding on to her against her will, and at the same time he was able to express, through the glove, something he couldn't express to her directly. So the object, in that sense, did it all."[2] In other words, the glove served Brando by allowing him to express through behavior the subtextual yearnings of the character. Because of his guilt for the role he played in Edie's brother's death at the start of the film, and because of his own sense of worthlessness, Terry does not feel permitted to express verbally his attraction for Edie. Brando found a way to express the character's desire behaviorally with the assistance of an object, and appreciative audiences thrilled at the virtuosity of the performance. Looking at the scene from another perspective, Paul Willemen and Noel King call it "epiphanic," which they define as providing revelations beyond the intention of the performance text and towards "an aspect or dimension of a person . . . which is not choreographed for you to see."[3] In phenomenological terms, something in excess of the character and the story became present in Brando's performance, even in the filmic medium.

In light of Bruce McConachie's admonition that theatre scholars apply cognitive research to their objects of inquiry whenever feasible, this article reevaluates the kinds of audience responses conjured by moments of performance like the white glove scene.[4] McConachie specifically cautions against relying upon twentieth-century critical theories like those reflected by Kazan and Willemen and King, but rather than reject those theories, he asks that they meet the demands of falsifiability—that is, that they be tried by the scientific method.[5] Yet, as David Saltz points out in his editorial comment to the *Theatre Journal* issue devoted to cognition, while McConachie tends to regard semiotic and phenomenological theories as "inadequate" to account for audience perception, other theatre scholars find that cognitive science may be used productively with other theoretical approaches, specifically phenomenology.[6] This paper argues that common ground exists between psychoanalytical, phenomenological, and neurological considerations of behavior, object use, and audience reception, especially in terms of their understanding of empathy, which is a touchstone issue of central concern to McConachie's work in cognition. The article seeks a better understanding of how various discourses inform our comprehension of the co-affection and empathic responses audiences experience during moments of heightened stage and film behavior.

Rather than simply extol further the virtues of cognitive science for theatre studies, however, this article also inserts cognitive studies, along with psychoanalysis and phenomenology, into another contemporary discourse currently transpiring on theory, spectatorship, and the unique essence of performance. Expressing disenchantment with the negative assessments of performance stated or implied in recent criticism, Aleksandra Wolska and Alice Rayner call for an attention to performance that appreciates its unique facility for breathing new life into old forms, for engaging the force of becoming, and for "launching into the territory of the radically unknown," not as bracketed off from our own messy and inchoate lives but as intimately interwoven with them.[7] Rayner calls the "ghost" of theatre the sense that we as individuals bring our own pasts, experiences, and stories to bear on the present of performance, and thereby the presence of performance becomes haunted.[8] What cognitive science and phenomenology yet have to account for, and what psychoanalysis continues to attempt, is the degree to which our own specific and individual desires and memories partake in the creative endeavors we encounter—like that of Brando, Saint, and a glove. Therefore, as Wolska suggests, citing Tadeusz Kantor, "To find performance as a mode of becoming, we have no choice but to look for it in the 'very manifestation of life.'"[9]

The article proceeds in two parts. The first defines the kind of prop use Brando demonstrates with the white glove in light of recent scholarship on stage props and within the American Method acting tradition generally in order to better understand the discourses that inform the authorial interpretation of the scene Kazan provides. Because the Method was greatly influenced by Freudian psychoanalysis and understood as a means for actors/characters to become present and transparent to audiences, the second part takes a closer look at how psychoanalysis and phenomenology account for the kinds of audience co-affection stage realism fosters and how cognitive studies corroborate those accounts. The article closes with summary thoughts about how further investigations might lead us into an appreciation of performance—and of props in performance—as a manifestation of each of our individual lives.

I. Props, Subtext, and the Method

What do audiences see in the white glove of the white glove scene? The first characteristic to note is its utter banality. Inexpensive, made of heavy cotton yarn, knitted, possibly store bought but not new, the glove complements the prim yet economically disadvantaged nature of its owner, Edie Doyle. The glove has no arresting quality of its own—no monogram, pattern, or detail, nothing to set it apart as unique. Were Brando not to have toyed with it we may have missed its presence in the performance frame altogether. In *The Stage Life of Props* (2003) Andrew Sofer focuses upon the degree to which props rise above what he calls their iconic (that is, intended) use in order to draw attention to themselves and thereby command an integral position within the play's narrative and sometimes outside the narrative as well. The white glove resists transcending its iconicity and banality, and therefore it distinguishes itself from the eight categories of prop use that Sofer outlines.

The glove is not a transformational object because in the hands of the actors it does not become, or signify, another object altogether. Audiences observe and understand Edie's white glove always as Edie's white glove even when it is on Terry's hand. Likewise the glove is not defamiliarized. The actors never use it so that it does not function as a glove and thereby do not tempt the audience to lose the narrative thread of the story in order to reassess the context in which the prop appears or to question the prop's nature. Because of Terry's unconscious handling of the glove it does seem to become fetishized; it becomes, in Sofer's words, "the focus of a character's projected desire, fear, or anxiety."[10] But in Sofer's description, a fetishized prop takes on the special significance invested by a character, maintains that significance for the audience for the duration of the play, and thereby rises to symbolic stature in association with the play's theme, like Hedda Gabler's pistols and the check in *A Raisin in the Sun*. In the case of *On the Waterfront,* the white glove takes on no more significance than what Terry invests in it only during the one scene. The use of the glove helps to advance the narrative without becoming a part of the narrative; the glove draws attention not to itself but to Terry, and likewise it avoids according with another of Sofer's categories, that of signifying independently of the actor who handles it.[11]

Therefore we may propose an additional category for Sofer's list: that props may maintain their iconic value while at the same time serve to reveal character subtext. This category divides into two subcategories. In the first, characters may use props *consciously* to express their subtext. As an example, in Tony Kushner's *Homebody/Kabul* (2001), Quango Twistleton, high on heroin, takes Priscilla Ceiling's panties from her suitcase and puts them on his head, then puts his head in the suitcase.[12] The behavior is done when nobody else is present (Priscilla's father is asleep on the bed having just smoked heroin) and reveals the extent of Quango's desperation, loneliness, and perversion. Similarly, in an early scene of Paula Vogel's *How I Learned to Drive* (1997), Uncle Peck offers his handkerchief to L'il Bit, who has been crying, so she can empty the content of her nose into it. After doing so she hands it back to Peck and, in Paula Vogel's words, "Without her seeing, he reverently puts it back."[13] The odd behavior—most people don't revere snotty handkerchiefs—reveals Peck's subtextual feelings for his seventeen-year-old niece.

In the above examples the characters are aware of their behavior and are intentional in its execution. Brando's use of the white glove provides an example of the second subcategory, that of a character using a prop *unconsciously* to express the character's subtext. As critics have surmised, Brando's behavior aims to communicate that Terry is unconscious of his handling of Edie's glove, and his unconscious activity speaks volumes about his unspoken feelings for Edie.[14] An early example of unconscious behavior with an object in modern drama occurs at the beginning of Heinrich von Kleist's *Prince Friedrich of Homburg* (1811). The Prince, on the eve of a decisive battle with the Swedish army, longs for success and recognition. Taking a rest at the castle of the Elector of Brandenburg before joining his troops for the march to battle, the Prince sleepwalks and, unconsciously, makes for himself a laurel wreath.[15] The behavior illuminates for the court the extent of the Prince's ambition, which turns out to be reckless and sets up the problem of the play.

While not transformed, defamiliarized, or fetishized, props used to reveal subtext acquire a special status that they do not have at any other time in the production or when they are used in a daily, utilitarian manner. The white glove scene would not have attained its singular status had Brando/Terry simply handed the glove back to Saint/Edie after she dropped it; layers of Quango's and Peck's emotional problems would remain hidden without the manipulation of panties and handkerchief; and without the laurel wreath, nobody would be able to gauge the Prince's inner thoughts. For brief moments subtextual behavior with a prop enriches the audience's comprehension of the verbal flow by revealing for the audience bursts of recognition of hidden facets of the character. Properties like gloves and handkerchiefs skirt the existential possibility that they partake in character agency because, as Rayner notes, "they are not metaphoric substitutes for the person but metonymic connections, attached by mutual touch."[16] Interest and enjoyment in the subtextual use of props stem not only from the audience's engaged construction of character and plot that the behavioral moments provide, but at times they also stem from what Willemen and King have identified as the reception of meanings that appear to be in excess of the intended meanings of the authors or actors and that seem to resonate intimately with individual spectators.

The white glove scene offers one notable case. Part of the excess has to do with the unique personal presence that Brando provides—his noted mystique and sexual allure across the gender divide. Furthermore, his acting reputation rests on his exhibition of a craft that makes seemingly improvised moments with mundane objects like a glove routine.[17] But another explanation for such excess might reside in the popular notion that Brando really was living, and not reproducing or manufacturing, his most startling moments of performance, that his acting realized the Method ideal of "being in the moment," and that he himself was unconscious of the behaviors he exhibited. As Krin Gabbard observes, "The variety of gestures that Brando explores with the glove, seemingly without artifice, convinced many that he was letting his unconscious do the work for him and that he was drawing on training based in psychological insights."[18]

James Naremore has labeled Brando's handling of the white glove as "a locus classicus of Method technique."[19] Yet he also argues that the Method should not be given too much credit for pioneering the psychological dimension of character behavior, given that neither the recognition of subtext nor the expressive use of objects were twentieth-century stage inventions, as evidenced in the example of *Prince Friedrich of Homburg* above. But more than that, the belief that Method training promotes a use of objects to reveal subtext is not supported by a review of the tenets of Method technique. None of the acting texts in the American tradition nor any that they spawned nor even the trilogy of acting instruction books by the Method's primary source of inspiration, Constantin Stanislavski, address a use of props beyond their intended utilitarian design.[20] The mention of props in these books simply serves to advance a truism of psychological realism: that actors inhabit the physical lives of their characters and in so doing exploit the behavioral possibilities inherent in all manner of stage props by, for example, reading a newspaper, tying shoelaces, and fiddling with desktop items.

Nonetheless, most practitioners working in realism would recognize the subtextual use of a prop as characteristic of realist acting despite its lack of mention in acting texts. They do so not only because authors like Kushner and Vogel insert tantalizing uses of properties in their stage directions, but because the subtextual use of a prop does not fall afield of the theoretical tenets of the Method. Steve Vineberg in *Method Actors: Three Generations of an American Acting Style* (1991) argues in detail what has been recognized as a critical commonplace for some time—that the Method, stimulated by Stanislavski's application of psychological insights, codified the psychoanalysis of Sigmund Freud (1856–1939) as the foundational principle of its acting process.[21] The Method in turn prepared actors to reveal through expression and behavior the unconscious and repressed problems of the characters who populated the plays of authors likewise influenced by Freud, such as Eugene O'Neill, Tennessee Williams, Arthur Miller, William Inge, and others.[22]

As the books devoted to expounding the Method reveal, the writers emphasize relaxation, sensory perception, improvisation, character appearance and mannerisms, and the availability of complex emotion. Most of these techniques aim to cultivate a type of acting that appears to be transpiring as if for the first time and in a manner that is truthful and available in a way that the presentational acting of the late nineteenth-century stage and early twentieth-century film was not. As the realist

American films of the midcentury demonstrate and preserve for us today, great stock was placed on how well an actor could reveal through subtlety of expression the problems of the character's past: Blanche's haunting by the death of her homosexual husband in *A Streetcar Named Desire* (1947), Biff's betrayal by his father in *Death of a Salesman* (1949), and the guilt and shame of the entire Tyrone family for its multiple skeletons in the closet in *Long Day's Journey into Night* (1942).[23] That the past loomed large in the psyche of a character reinforced a central Freudian hypothesis, that the problems and neuroses of the individual result from repressed unconscious drives that war against the subject's ego.[24] Moreover, the sources of such problems—or the nature of the unconscious drives—become evident to the psychoanalyst (and informed spectator) through slips of tongue, unconscious behaviors, and other revealing symptoms such as dreams.

While the Method primers neglect discussing unconscious behaviors in detail and subtextual behaviors with objects altogether, Freud provides definitions and examples. In *Psychopathology of Everyday Life* (1901), Freud distinguishes two types of behavior that reveal unconscious desires and motives. Of note, while Freud does not draw attention to this, most of the examples he provides entail a telling use of a mundane object. The first, "bungled actions," are behaviors routinely executed successfully (like locking the door when leaving the house) but for some reason executed poorly or unsuccessfully on noteworthy occasions (like forgetting to lock the door when leaving the house for several days). The second type of behaviors Freud called "symptomatic and chance actions." These are distinguished from bungled actions because they are not variants of habitual behaviors but are unique occurrences that nonetheless do not draw attention to themselves because they seem innocent (like cutting your ring finger accidentally on your wedding anniversary). As with every uncharacteristic action in the life of human beings, Freud places psychoanalytic value on both bungled actions and symptomatic and chance actions; in all cases they reveal something of the unconscious life of the individual.[25]

Actors aware of the subtextual possibilities available to them in the unconscious handling of mundane objects can create behavioral moments that reinforce or exceed the specific demands of the playwright. The blind character Don in Leonard Gershe's *Butterflies Are Free* (1969) demonstrates throughout the play that he can navigate his apartment as well as any sighted person. At the climax of the play, he attempts to communicate to Jill that he does not feel hurt by her standing him up for a candlelit dinner and leaving him for another man, and he nonchalantly eats a corned beef sandwich. Gershe provides some clichéd stage directions that illuminate Don's pain, such as stammering through lines of dialogue and bumping into things—the kinds of behaviors many journeymen playwrights and actors might invent.[26] But imagine that as the actor/Don eats his sandwich, he reaches for a glass of water but picks up instead a lit candle and lifts it to his mouth, only to set it back down quickly with embarrassment when he feels the heat of the flame against his face. In his distracted state, the actor/Don loses the composure and physical dexterity he normally exhibits, commits a bungled action and almost burns himself, and unconsciously reveals to Jill and the audience the level of his inner torment.

George in Arthur Miller's *All My Sons* (1947) arrives at the Kellers' backyard after having visited his father in prison for the first time in several years. In a scene that lasts no more than fifteen minutes, the actor playing in a realistic mode must chart an incredibly difficult arc of the character's experience even though the text provides no behavioral cues.[27] He must arrive in an outrage bent on disrupting the proposed marriage between his sister Ann and Chris Keller, then within the span of a few minutes acquiesce to the warmth of the Keller family, and then become enraged again once Kate Keller reveals her husband Joe's culpability in sending George's father to jail. As George greets Chris and Ann with emotional distance as the stage directions indicate, imagine that the actor adds to George's attitude the shock of a flood of delightful childhood memories that war against his recently awakened indignation. As he avoids Chris and Ann, the actor/George distractedly approaches the arbor, picks a leaf from a vine, crushes it and smells it. The aroma triggers memories and feelings from an idyllic but lost past. Even before the actor/George begins his argument with Chris and Ann, and before Chris's mother, Kate, can work her charm on him, the physical environment softens his resolve to confront Joe. Later in the scene as his old girlfriend Lydia, who is now married to someone else, leaves, the actor/George offers her a glass of Kate's grape drink or an apple sitting in a basket nearby in a desperate attempt to keep her in the backyard, which she declines. All of the actions are chance and symptomatic actions that could be interpreted as innocent and empty of intent but are full of meaning on the subtextual level and reveal George's emotional fragility.

Spectators watching such behavioral moments proposed above or those exhibited by Brando with the glove indeed may be interpreting the performances according to dominant discourses that their culture provides.[28] Because the language of psychoanalysis has permeated the North American landscape of the late twentieth century as well as the emergent twenty-first, spectators likely receive and interpret the behaviors with objects as unconscious and as communicating meanings that support and also exceed the demands of the performance texts.[29] But what accounts for the sensation that the revelation of character or actor in such behavioral moments—a revelation that author, director, or even actor may not anticipate—strikes one as personal, private, or even epiphanic? As explored below, cognitive science informs us of the degree to which the individuals in the audience are likely to be feeling remarkably similar physical sensations and emotions, and may be sharing intensely empathic responses to the characters. But as Rayner points out, sometimes the ineffable quality of performance does not transpire unless audiences bring "a certain mode of attention," that is, that they join in the creation of performance. She continues, "The consciousness of performance is impossible without the performers, the materiality of the stage, the audience, the moment. Such consciousness is not *in* any of them, yet arises from them and in a certain sense because of their intersection."[30] The mundane prop at times lies at the heart of the intersection, and we attach to it not only the stories of the text or of the character but those of ourselves.

II. Props, Neurons, and Empathy

The word *Einfühlung*, literally "in-feeling" or "feeling into" but translated as "empathy," was coined in 1873 by the German philosopher Robert Vischer (1847–1933) as a means to explain human emotion in relation to aesthetic appreciation. Vischer used it to describe the feelings human beings receive when they project themselves into the inanimate forms they encounter in the world, like cliffs and buildings. By projecting myself into the size and expanse of a mountain, for example, I receive in turn the emotional sensation of grandeur and aspiration.[31] Another German philosopher, Theodor Lipps (1851–1914), applied the term to psychology in order to explain our awareness that other people also have selves, and he ranks empathy as one prime source of knowledge, the other two being sense perception and inner perception.[32] Lipps's consideration of the term influenced both Freud and the phenomenologist Edmund Husserl (1859–1938) who saw empathy as one means by which people can extend their consciousness into that of another person and thereby come into the fullest knowledge possible of the other.

From the phenomenological perspective, to empathize with another means to extend my understanding away from myself in order to experience the life of another, and I do this by means of an intuitive act; I allow the being of the other to be totally present to me. Because of our shared co-humanity I can associate the psychic life of another and enter into it. Notably, the extension into another's life happens through the sensory perception of the other. As J. N. Mohanty writes, "In the other's bodily *expressions* I visibly perceive the other's inner life."[33] In so doing, I then come to understand better the view of the world from another's subjective perspective and I understand better a set of actions that at first seem foreign or confusing to me. I experience, through empathy, "the mental life, the consciousness, of another I—not in the same way I experience mine, but in another, very different, manner." In empathy I am taken from my own life and placed within another life and I experience it as it is, without judging it or "bestowing meaning upon it" as I do objects.[34]

To feel empathy for another does not mean to sympathize with another; empathy is not grounded primarily in shared feelings or shared sentiments. I may find after I empathize with another that my view of the world, different from the other's, makes better sense for me. I even may disagree with actions taken by another, but at least after the experience of empathy I have a greater understanding of the other and might be better equipped to hold the other in an inclusive ethical regard. Likewise, empathy should not be confused with pity, for when I feel pity for another I have already made a value judgment that the other suffers some kind of lack and therefore is in need of some kind of emotional support from me. To empathize does not mean I must form some kind of relationship with the other. Rather, to empathize means that I can fully feel with the other, maintain my own sense of self, and grant to the other equal subjectivity. Husserl labels as "appresentation" the sense that I can experience the presence of another subject as well as my own *at the same time*.[35] Furthermore, in our empathy for others comes the greater realization that the world we inhabit is constituted *intersubjectively,* that is, that the world is created and constituted not only by me and my own understanding but by all other subjects as well.[36]

Freud's conception of empathy remains closer to Lipps's formulation and, while Freud does not enter an engaged critique of empathy, he sees it as a means for us to understand others by putting ourselves in their place. He also thinks empathy essential for the analyst to adopt in order to understand patients during treatment.[37] Cognitive science has indeed invalidated many of Freud's hypotheses such as the structural and topographical models of consciousness, the Oedipus and Electra complexes, and the two drives of eros and thanatos. But as contemporary psychologists argue, Freud remains relevant to the degree that most of our cognitive processes are unconscious and that, though yet to be explained satisfactorily by neuroscience, the clinical setting works to relieve individuals of psychic stress.[38] By the end of the twentieth century, empathy had maintained its status as a primary tool of the psychoanalyst's craft, and the ethical implication of empathy in phenomenology has found its way into contemporary neuroscience, specifically in its accounting for the evolution of human beings as social animals.[39]

With the aid of functional magnetic resonance imaging (fMRI), neurologists for the past decade and a half have been able to conduct empirical research on all manner of neurological phenomena. As McConachie argues in more depth, studies in the neurological processes of empathy provide a framework for understanding the emotional experience of spectators at performance.[40] In one example, Philip Jackson, Andrew Meltzoff, and Jean Decety showed test subjects pictures that inferred the infliction of pain on others and asked them to rate the level of pain the people in the pictures might feel (see figure 3). They noted increased activity in areas of the brain known to play significant roles in the processing of one's own pain (the anterior cingulate, the anterior insula, the cerebellum, and to a lesser extent the thalamus), and that the activity in one specific brain area strongly correlated with the participants' ratings of the others' pain (the anterior cingulate). They conclude from this test and others like it that "the feeling of pain is not restricted to its physical sensation, but occurs within the individual as a result of observing another's emotional state." They ventured that empathy transpires with a degree of emotional identification given that a person exhibits "an affective response to another person, which often, but not always, entails sharing that person's emotional state." They also recognize a conscious identification because their subjects demonstrated "a cognitive capacity to take the perspective of the other person while keeping self and other differentiated."[41] The "appresentation" that Husserl posits seems to be corroborated by the observation that the test subjects could feel with and understand others while maintaining a secure sense of themselves, their physical safety, and their lack of pain.

The presence of properties in figure 3 are so banal as to practically escape notice. The four compositions represent mundane situations and all could classify as one of Freud's bungled actions. In all four situations, the subject of the photograph is not passive but active, that is, negotiating a car door or slicing a cucumber. Given that action is implied in the still photographs, the situations invite narrative interpretation—a story of some type seems to transpire in each. Because the first-person perspective of the photographs comes close to positioning the viewer as the agent of the event, the implied action implicates the viewer within the narrative, and it may not be difficult for observers to envision the slicing of their own index finger with a knife and then dribbling the white cutting board and translucent cucumber with crimson blood. In this regard the banal properties—a doorknob, a knife, a cucumber—firmly situate the subjects of the photos as engaged in a physical, social world.

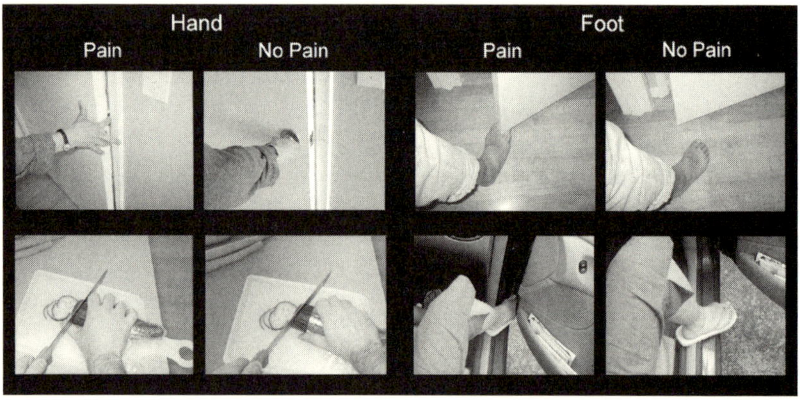

Photographs suggesting pain. Reprinted from *NeuroImage* 24 (2005), Philip Jackson, Andrew Meltzoff, and Jean Decety, "How Do We Perceive the Pain of Others? A Window into the Neural Processes Involved in Empathy," 773. Used by permission of Elsevier.

The objects add an embodied layer of meaning that simple vocal, facial, and bodily expressions cannot summon. And in order to understand the narratives, we bring our own experiences to bear in the telling.

McConachie discusses the discovery by neuroscience of "mirror neurons" as an unconscious cognitive means by which human beings attend to, understand, and anticipate the behaviors and use of objects by others.[42] Described by Vittorio Gallese, mirror neurons are neurons in the brain that discharge not only when we execute actions but also when we observe others executing the same or similar actions. Mirror neurons are not isolated in the brain but connect to the physical extremities via the motor system, that is, the neurological pathways that descend from the brain to the rest of the body. Gallese proposes, with the support of other studies, that the existence of mirror neurons "could be at the basis of a direct form of action understanding."[43]

In an fMRI study conducted by Gallese and colleagues, participants observed videos that represented contexts for action (a tidy tea service and a messy tea service), actions without context (a hand grasping a cup two different ways), and actions within a context, or what the researchers label as "intention" (a hand grasping a cup to drink or to clean up a mess) (see figure 4).[44] The videos for actions without context and intention, but not for context alone, activated the right frontal cortex areas of the brain, which are known to be part of the mirror neuron system, and the videos for intention elicited even stronger neural responses than those for action without context. The results led the researchers to con-

Six Images Taken from the Context, Action, and Intention Clips. From Iacoboni, et al. "Grasping the Intentions of Others with One's Own Mirror Neuron System," *PLoS Biology* 3, no. 3 (March 2005): 529–33.

clude that the mirror neuron system assists human beings in understanding and anticipating the actions of others. Comprehension of the actions and motives of others does not occur only as conscious mental activities. Our bodies inform us of the intentions of others. As Gallese writes, "Such body-related experiential knowledge enables a direct grasping of the sense of the actions performed by others, and of the emotions and sensations they experience."[45]

Whereas the mirror neuron system allows us to attune to others and shows that through empathy we understand others better, cognitive science and phenomenology have yet to address the extent to which, in our modeling of others, we attune others—specifically the characters/actors in performance—to ourselves. Likewise what remains unexplored is the extent to which in our modeling of others in performance we become more attuned to ourselves as well. As Wolska claims, "performance cares not for the end, but grows through it into other forms of continuance. It transforms the world into a theatre where a show is but one phase in a process that goes on continuously in real life."[46] As the mirror neuron system and processes for empathy clarify, we take ourselves and our histories into performance, and through our experiences we participate in the creation of the theatre event. But in addition, the theatre event accompanies us into our future lives and serves to inform our becoming. The objects that litter our world play a significant role in our understanding of character and performance because, as Rayner observes, "The historical, memorial, and nostalgic functions of objects are possible because objects already relate to humans through a paradox of intimacy and exclusion."[47] The paradox exists because characters, actors, and spectators all bring their own intersubjective histories to bear in the intersections of performance. Our commonality in part stems from our shared existence in a physical world and our shared manipulation of the objects that make up that world.

Current studies in consciousness and neurology challenge our assumptions about the affective and "excessive" aspects of performance and provide the foundation for an empirical and materialist theory of audience reception that McConachie and others have begun to pioneer.[48] Various critics have looked at unique behavioral moments of performance like Brando's handling of a white glove and attempted to account for the apparent communication of meanings in excess of the performance text or even the performers' intentions. Twentieth-century phenomenology and psychoanalysis offered several theories toward the recognition of an individual's interior state. Vischer's and Lipps's recognition of the human attribute of empathy served both disciplines by providing an explanation for how one subject could experience the physical sensations, thoughts, and feelings of another. Contemporary cognitive studies into empathy and the discovery of a mirror neuron system seem to confirm that the human body has the innate ability to share the subjective experience of another by literally making the other present to one's self through shared feelings and physical sensations. Still, the meanings or revelations identified as transpiring in performance in excess of authorial intention may still resist our theoretical attempts to explain them, especially to the degree that performance speaks to us individually. But one observation surfaces—that the mutual realities of our lives and the theatre coalesce in a tactile world of objects.

Notes

Research for the article was funded in part by the University of Kentucky Research Foundation, the College of Fine Arts, and the Department of Theatre. Special thanks to Les Wade and John Lehne.

1. Budd Schulberg, *On the Waterfront* (Carbondale: Southern Illinois University Press, 1980), 47–50.

2. Michel Ciment, *Kazan on Kazan* (New York: Viking Press, 1974), 46.

3. Paul Willemen, *Looks and Frictions: Essays in Cultural Studies and Film Theory* (Bloomington: Indiana University Press, 1994), 235, 237.

4. Bruce McConachie, *Engaging Audiences: A Cognitive Approach to Spec-*

tating in the Theatre (New York: Palgrave Macmillan, 2008), 3–8; McConachie, "Falsifiable Theories for Theatre and Performance Studies," *Theatre Journal* 59, no. 4 (2007): 553–56.

5. McConachie, *Engaging Audiences,* 8–9; McConachie, "Falsifiable Theories," 571.

6. David Z. Saltz, "Editorial Comment: Performance and Cognition," *Theatre Journal* 59, no. 4 (2007).

7. Aleksandra Wolska, "Rabbits, Machines, and the Ontology of Performance," *Theatre Journal* 57, no. 1 (2005): 84; Alice Rayner, *Ghosts: Death's Double and the Phenomena of Theatre* (Minneapolis: University of Minnesota Press, 2006), xx.

8. Rayner, *Ghosts,* xix.

9. Wolska, "Rabbits, Machines, and the Ontology of Performance," 88.

10. Andrew Sofer, *The Stage Life of Props* (Ann Arbor: University of Michigan Press, 2003), 23.

11. See Sofer's discussion of the eight categories of prop use (*Stage Life of Props,* 23–28).

12. Tony Kushner, *Homebody/Kabul* (New York: Theatre Communications Group, 2004), 103.

13. Paula Vogel, *How I Learned to Drive,* in *The Mammary Plays* (New York: Theatre Communications Group, 1998), 19.

14. Krin Gabbard, *Black Magic: White Hollywood and African American Culture* (New Brunswick, NJ: Rutgers University Press, 2004), 27; Andrew Higson, "Acting Taped: Andrew Higson Discusses a New Project on Cinema Performance with Mark Nash and James Swinson," *Screen: The Journal of the Society for Education in Film and Television* 26, no. 5 (September–October 1985): 12. See also Sam B. Girgus, *Hollywood Renaissance: The Cinema of Democracy in the Era of Ford, Capra, and Kazan,* (Cambridge, UK: Cambridge University Press, 1998), 159–60.

15. Heinrich von Kleist, *Prince Friedrich of Homburg,* trans. Diana Stone Peters and Frederick G. Peters (New York: New Directions, 1978), 5–9.

16. Rayner, *Ghosts,* 81.

17. Jonathan Jones goes so far as to call Brando's idiosyncratic use of objects "redundant" in "Brando, Pollock and Parker: The Wild Ones of American Art," *Guardian* (December 11, 2004), 61.

18. Gabbard, *Black Magic,* 27. See also Brian Neve, "*On the Waterfront,*" *History Today* 45, no. 6 (1995): 23.

19. James Naremore, *Acting in the Cinema* (Berkeley: University of California Press, 1990), 194. Naremore attributes the sentiment to Andrew Higson, but in Higson's discussion he cites the behavior as a means to focus actor concentration, which is a far cry from the kind of psychological subtext Naremore discusses. See Higson, "Acting Taped," 12.

20. Among the authors who do not mention a subtextual use of props are Stella Adler, Robert Barton, Robert Benedetti, Michael Chekhov, Robert Cohen, Uta Hagen, Lorraine Hull, Robert Lewis, Constantin Stanislavski, and Lee Strasberg. This list is not exhaustive. It follows that scholarship on Method acting onstage and film likewise neglects the subtextual use of props. For a recent example

see Cynthia Baron and Sharon Marie Carnicke, *Reframing Screen Performance* (Ann Arbor: University of Michigan Press, 2008), chapter 9, "Stanislavsky: Players' Actions as a Window into Characters' Interactions." The only mention of the subtextual use of a prop that I could find was the citation of the white glove scene (what else?) by Actors Studio alumnus John Lehne in Eva Mekler, *The New Generation of Acting Teachers* (New York: Penguin Books, 1988), 241–42. While Kazan never wrote an acting book, he does spend three paragraphs on the subtextual use of props in Ciment, *Kazan on Kazan,* 45–46.

21. Stanislavski was influenced by Ivan Pavlov (1849–1936) and Théodule Ribot (1839–1916).

22. Steve Vineberg, *Method Actors: Three Generations of an American Acting Style* (New York: Schirmer Books, 1991), 85–141.

23. I agree with Naremore that an "expressive-realist" style of acting was more of a general trend in early twentieth-century acting and not the exclusive purview of the Method (Naremore, *Acting in the Cinema,* 198). Note that Vivian Leigh, Blanche of the film version of *Streetcar,* was not a Method-trained actor, yet her performance could be mistaken for being Method influenced.

24. For an introduction to Freud's thought, see William W. Meissner, *Freud and Psychoanalysis* (Notre Dame: University of Notre Dame Press, 2000).

25. Sigmund Freud, *The Standard Edition of the Complete Psychological Works of Sigmund Freud,* vol. 6, *The Psychopathology of Everyday Life,* trans. James Strachey (London: Hogarth Press, 1960), 162–67, 191–201, 257.

26. Leonard Gershe, *Butterflies Are Free* (New York: Samuel French, 1969), 71–78.

27. Arthur Miller, *Eight Plays* (Garden City, NY: Nelson Doubleday, 1981), 56–74.

28. See, for example, Susan Bennett, *Theatre Audiences: A Theory of Production and Reception* (London: Routledge, 1990), 114, and McConachie, *Engaging Audiences,* chapter 2.

29. W. B. Worthen in *Modern Drama and the Rhetoric of Theater* (Berkeley: University of California Press, 1992) proposes that the Method provides North American audiences with the dominant discourse to interpret realist performance in the manner suggested by Susan Bennett (Bennett, *Theatre Audiences,* 52). I do not mean to say that psychoanalytic and phenomenological interpretations are the only two available. For feminist, Christian, and sociological interpretations of the white glove scene, see, respectively, Jeffrey Chown, "Visual Coding and Social Class in *On the Waterfront,*" in *On the Waterfront,* ed. Joanna E. Rapf (Cambridge: Cambridge University Press, 2003), 116; Neil P. Hurley, "*On the Waterfront:* Rebirth of a Contenduh," in *Image and Likeness: Religious Visions in American Film Classics,* ed. John R. May (Mahwah, NJ: Paulist Press, 1992), 99; and Kenneth R. Hey, "Ambivalence as a Theme in *On the Waterfront* (1954): An Interdisciplinary Approach to Film Study," in *Hollywood as Historian: American Film in a Cultural Context,* ed. Peter C. Rollins (Lexington: University Press of Kentucky, 1983), 178.

30. Rayner, *Ghosts,* xvii; emphasis in original.

31. Robert Vischer, "On the Optical Sense of Form: A Contribution to Aes-

thetics," in *Empathy, Form, and Space: Problems in German Aesthetics, 1873–1893,* intro. and trans. Harry Francis Mallgrave and Eleftherios Ikonomou (Santa Monica: Getty Center for the History of Art and the Humanities, 1994), 104–5.

32. G. W. Pigman, "Freud and the History of Empathy," *International Journal of Psychoanalysis* 76, no. 2 (April 1995): 240, 242.

33. J. N. Mohanty, *The Philosophy of Edmund Husserl: A Historical Development* (New Haven, CT: Yale University Press, 2008), 283; emphasis in original.

34. Ibid., 286, 287.

35. Edmund Husserl, *Cartesian Meditations: An Introduction to Phenomenology,* trans. Dorion Cairns (The Hague: Martinus Nijhoff, 1960), 109.

36. Dermot Moran, *Edmund Husserl: Founder of Phenomenology* (Cambridge, UK: Polity Press, 2005), 222–23.

37. Pigman, "Freud and the History of Empathy," 245–46.

38. See Wilma Bucci, *Psychoanalysis and Cognitive Science: A Multiple Code Theory* (New York: Guilford Press, 1997); Mauricio Cortina and Giovanni Liotti, "New Approaches to Understanding Unconscious Processes: Implicit and Explicit Memory Systems," *International Forum of Psychoanalysis* 16 (2007): 204–12; Soren R. Ekstrom, "The Mind beyond Our Immediate Awareness: Freudian, Jungian, and Cognitive Models of the Unconscious," *Journal of Analytical Psychology* 49 (2004): 657–82.

39. See Arthur C. Bohart and Leslie S. Greenberg, eds., *Empathy Reconsidered: New Directions in Psychotherapy* (Washington, DC: American Psychological Association, 1997); Martin L. Hoffman, *Empathy and Moral Development* (Cambridge, UK: Cambridge University Press, 2000); Jean Decety and Meghan Meyer, "From Emotion Resonance to Empathic Understanding: A Social Developmental Neuroscience Account," *Development and Psychopathology* 20 (2008): 1053–80.

40. See McConachie, *Engaging Audiences,* chapter 2, "Social Cognition in Spectating."

41. Philip Jackson, Andrew Meltzoff, and Jean Decety, "How Do We Perceive the Pain of Others? A Window into the Neural Processes Involved in Empathy," *NeuroImage* 24 (2005): 776, 771.

42. McConachie, *Engaging Audiences,* 70–87.

43. Vittorio Gallese, "Embodied Simulation: From Mirror Neuron Systems to Interpersonal Relations," in *Empathy and Fairness,* ed. Greg Bock and Jamie Goode (Chichester, UK: John Wiley and Sons, 2007), 5–6.

44. Marco Iacoboni, Istvan Molnar-Szakacs, Vittorio Gallese, Giovanni Buccino, John C. Mazziotta, Giacomo Rizzolatti, "Grasping the Intentions of Others with One's Own Mirror Neuron System," *PLoS Biology* 3, no. 3 (March 2005): 529–33.

45. Gallese, "Embodied Simulation," 9.

46. Wolska, "Rabbits, Machines, and the Ontology of Performance," 92.

47. Rayner, *Ghosts,* 79.

48. See also the essays collected in Bruce McConachie and F. Elizabeth Hart, eds., *Performance and Cognition: Theatre Studies and the Cognitive Turn* (London: Routledge, 2006).

From Props to Affordances

An Ecological Approach to Theatrical Objects

Teemu Paavolainen

> In the subject-oriented criticism inaugurated by Aristotle, stage objects either remain at the bottom of the hierarchy of theatrical elements deemed worthy of analysis . . . or else drop out of critical sight altogether.
>
> —Andrew Sofer

LOOKING AT how scenography has traditionally been conceptualized, we basically find two levels of abstraction and analysis: one concerned with "objects"—a theoretical, detached, and fairly recent concern—and one, with the more pragmatic vocabulary of scenery, props, and perhaps costumes. A proponent of the former, semiotician Patrice Pavis notes the "difficulty of drawing a definite boundary between the actor and the surrounding world" as a basis for using *object* as the analytical term—one he finds "neutral [and] empty," as opposed to the baggage of tradition carried by *props* or *scenery.* Part of a "Western cultural heritage," he deems the latter terms "classical," or even "antiquated," and in the event of performance, these alleged categories do indeed easily morph into one another, as many a theatre scholar has effectively argued. A bit of costume may occasionally turn into a prop, and a chair will only remain a bit of "scenery" until drawn into the action itself; as Manfred Pfister aptly puts it, any object may "shift from one position to another within the structural spectrum of 'figure-costume-property-set.'" In other words still, none of these positions can really be "delimited as a closed sphere," any more than can the very categories of *actor* and *object,* in the end. This is how the issue was framed in 1940, already, by the Prague School semiotician Jiří Veltruský. Advocating an idea of a living continuum over any fixed categories, he found the above kind of fluctuation a matter of actors and objects alike (set, props, and costume) gaining and shedding what he enigmatically called their "action force."[1]

Veltruský's concept has been deservedly influential. In what comes closest to a definition, he says this force "attracts a certain action" to the prop or whatever has such, and "provokes in us the expectation of [that] action." Dynamic by nature, it also emerges as relative to what he calls "the static forces of characterization," predominant when a dagger, for instance, merely appears as part of a costume. In the dynamic context of stabbing someone, it exhibits its action force and "becomes a prop," functioning as "a sign of murder" thereafter. For historian of props Andrew Sofer, however, this appears "murky" and too universal for distinguishing stage objects from stage subjects. Equating Veltruský's concept with "semiotic subjectivity," Sofer thus arrives at much the same boundary syndrome as did Pavis, earlier. For a different line of interpretation, still, Gay McAuley refers action force to what anthropologist Marcel Jousse dubs "the gesture of things"—that "we really know things only to the extent that they perform or 'gestualise' themselves in us"—and suggests this goes beyond action force: instead of just creating expectations or (passively) participating in action, objects "contain their own gestural demands" and actually impose behavior on actors. In Sofer's refreshingly sober analysis, finally, objects only "become props" when physically manipulated by actors: regardless of their size or portability or whatever other conceivable conditions, "wherever a prop exists, an actor-object interaction exists." With motion as the prop's "defining feature," he denies their having any "underlying logic" other than "what Wittgenstein called a family resemblance."[2]

As these examples should suffice to attest, then, there cannot really be any objectively necessary and sufficient *properties* to stage properties—as is often the case with human categories, more generally, the boundaries are inescapably fuzzy. Just think of comedy and tragedy: we're sure that the central examples are very different, but there's clearly gray area in between. In cognitive theories of categorization (drawing explicitly on Wittgenstein's insights) such central members of categories have been termed "prototypes." For example, furniture and tools would be clearer cases of *artifacts* than buildings or bread, the whole category defined only by family resemblance. Likewise, props could be considered prototypical of theatrical objects—Veltruský's continuum, allowing a degree of creativity to our fuzzying up or extending their conceptual boundaries—but then again, I wouldn't expect even most theatre people to have a clear prototype for the overall category of props, given its level of abstraction. Just as we cannot interact with or purchase or draw or visualize a "general piece of furniture" (one that isn't a chair, a table, or a bed, for instance), we cannot do those things to a prop in general. On what is considered a cognitively basic level—one at which category members look much more alike and call for similar interactions (contrast *chairs* with furniture or beanbags)—we would have to think of particular props and the particular motions that make them props, under Sofer's definition.[3]

Following linguist George Lakoff, such basic levels of human categorization could neatly be called "human-sized," in that the properties of concern are not inherent to the objects as much as they are *interactional*. While it may be hard to think of particular prototypes for parts of the set, props, or costumes, they do call for different kinds of basic-level interaction. As for theatrical objects, then, an advisable first step might be to "zoom out" from the concepts themselves, to the kinds of relationships they inhere in—with acting and movement, say—or, to enlarge on Sofer's definition, to situations of "actor-object interaction" including, but not restricted to, the manipulation of stage props. To suggest such a step, this essay will introduce an approach known as *ecological psychology* and, specifically, its central concept of *affordances*, coined by the American perceptual psychologist James J. Gibson (1904–79). Befitting my subject matter, "ecology," here, should be understood in the highly inclusive terms of *organism-environment interaction*, that is, as substantially extending what we could term the prototypical conception of its domain, as "a natural biological science distinct from the human social sciences."[4] Affordances, accordingly, would be specific situations of such interaction, whether we choose to consider it natural, cultural, or theatrical. In the course of the essay, I will try to demonstrate how the term can serve to relativize not only the unwarranted generality or specificity of concepts such as *object* or *prop*, respectively, but the very dichotomy of subjects and objects (grounding Sofer's worries about "semiotic subjectivity") and how it can be used to productively modify Veltruský's ideas of "action force."

Finally, as my brief account of categorization suggests, the larger context for all of this is in the emerging field of cognitive studies in theatre and performance[5]—but it comes with a twist: in ecological terms, agency and cognition cannot be explained away by reducing them to the neural workings of the brain alone. As the prototypical applications of affordance theory concern the use of material objects, however, such more philosophical implications can only be approached layer upon layer, as it were. In the first part of the essay, I will discuss how stage objects "afford" theatrical action, and how such an approach affords analyzing them in terms of this action rather than such confining categories as set or props. Subsequently, a tentative layering is proposed from *intentional*, *immediate*, and *improvised* affordances, to how all of these may afford *interpretations*, for the critic or spectator—the range is wide, to be sure, but on the ecological account, anything onstage will not likely "mean" just anything. While some of this discussion will already draw on cognitive metaphor theory, the concluding remarks on agency and cognition derive again from Veltruský's proposal that we should not think of agents and objects as "closed spheres," to begin with. Only when we deconstruct their dichotomical definitions into ones of ecological interimplication do we stand a chance of "elevating" props and other kinds of stage objects to the same level of academic interest as the actors and other theatrical elements "deemed worthy of analysis," in Sofer's opening quotation. To summarize my own agenda on Gibson, finally, his approach has been beautifully applied to film and music, already, but as for theatre studies (a few important nods aside), a major opening still awaits. In the bounds of our topic, this essay is an attempt to provide one.[6]

Steps to an Ecology of Performance

A preliminary definition of affordances can be taken from Gibson himself: "The affordances of the environment are what it *offers* the animal, what it *provides* or *furnishes,* either for good or ill. The verb *to afford* is found in the dictionary, but the noun *affordance* is not. I have made it up. I mean by it something that refers to both the environment and the animal in a way that no existing term does. It implies the complementarity of the animal and the environment."[7] Put simply, then, affordances are what one can do with things, their functional meanings or values for an individual, or the possibilities for interaction in an environment—more to do with verbs than nouns, in a sense, but always in terms of a basic, ecological fittedness of agent and world (including that of actors and objects, in the theatre). Indeed, this idea of a fundamental mutuality or reciprocity characterizes Gibson's very understanding of ecology as well as perception. Tightly interwoven with action, "direct perception" equals one's continuous awareness of both the environment and of oneself, and especially of the affordances of their ongoing functional relationship. "Environment," consequently, is for Gibson not the objective, abstract reality of physics or geometry, but an ecological one, specified in relation to the organism it surrounds and the interactions their relationship affords. Yet it is a profoundly meaningful environment: "information," in the Gibsonian brand of direct realism, need not be added to arbitrary stimuli, but only picked up by perceptual systems attuned to what he calls the "invariant" aspects of surrounding reality. Affordances, consequently, would be "compound invariants," the functional meaning of which we likely perceive even more directly than we do their individual components. Specified by "an edge with an acute dihedral angle," what we likely attend to in Veltruský's dagger is the "compound" that specifies the range of its action force. Likewise, it might take some conceptual labor to analyze an object into a "horizontal, flat, and rigid" surface, "knee-high above the ground," instead of just perceiving that it affords sitting on.[8]

Unlike physical properties, thus, affordances only emerge in *situated interaction* within a given ecology, relative to an acting organism whether this be an individual or a species. For fish, water serves as a medium for living and breathing and moving within; for us, as a substance to drink or swim in or wash ourselves with. In high epistemological terms, the concept is "both physical and psychical, yet neither," cutting across the subjective and the objective: "What a thing *is* and what it *means* are not separate, the former being physical and the latter mental as we are accustomed to believe."[9] Compared to your standard semiotics, then, such an ecological theory of meaning will tolerate—even presuppose—a whole lot of unintended signs besides the intentional: the action force or affordance of the dagger will be perceived immediately (Veltruský's "expectation of action") and can then be actualized or not, given the reciprocity of perception and action—and note it does afford more than "stabbing."

Now, let us consider the practical implications of this. For one, simple material objects can simultaneously afford very different actions for different individuals, or indeed for the same individual at different times: functioning as a "trap" for Tartuffe, in Molière's play, Orgon's table obviously affords hiding, for the latter. Understood as features of a *relationship,* affordances do not "cause" or "impose" action in some behavioristic manner (as for Jousse), but only make it possible within a very precise set of constraints, both environmental and individual. Thus, a given prop's affordances are surely not only a matter of its physical form and size: the "knee-high" aspect of sitting, for example, can be perceived only with a proprioceptive awareness of one's own height and leg length. Reciprocally, the perception of any environmental affordance will always involve the "coperception" of one's relevant bodily proportions: in *Waiting for Godot,* the tree appears too weak for Didi and Gogo to hang themselves and too narrow to hide behind, given their weight and width. And of course, hanging oneself or stabbing someone makes little sense unless taken in a context of intentional action—phenomenologically, as Harry Heft has argued, we need to define affordances with respect to each agent's "intentional repertoire," and not her body alone. Finally, embodiment, skill, and intentionality alike are constrained by age, experience, and perceptual learning. Keeping with Heft, as the motor abilities and intentional capacities of an individual change, "the affordances of the environment change concurrently," whole fields of affordances opening up and closing down, with development, aging, or, indeed, theatrical training. In bodily terms alone, a bar stool doesn't afford sitting for a very young infant, nor does a cardboard box for a slightly older and heavier person.[10]

All these ecological variables considered, it is little short of redundant to speak of objects "becoming props," as do both Veltruský and Sofer, let alone of things becoming objects, as does McAuley. As Freddie Rokem points out in his critique of overly linguistic theatre semiotics, the materiality of theatrical objects remains even as they come to signify different things—what can and will change, we could add, is their relationship with the actors, that is, their affordances either actual or "performed." Indeed, as the psychologist Heft argues, a functional classification of environmental features may illuminate attributes that purely form-based taxonomies are bound to miss, mask, or conflate. Intuitive and obvious as it may appear to categorize features as "mold-able" or "climb-on-able" (in terms of their affordances), it remains an ecological fact that "not all trees afford the same activity"—nor, of course, do props. What these considerations afford in our present discussion, then, is questioning Pavis's definition of *object* as "neutral or empty," and extending Sofer's idea of *props* as affording actual motion. Although they both count as objects and can be used as props, a brick and a rope will inevitably afford different kinds of motions—ones, moreover, that also implicate the actors' movements. Quite traditionally, a "psychologically meaningful" distinction we might thus consider is between the affordances of what Gibson calls *attached* and *detached* objects, in that the former (attached, like much of prototypical scenery) articulate possibilities for locomotion—paths and barriers, enclosures and occluding surfaces—but not for manipulation, at least not in the fairly unrestricted sense afforded by detached objects that are also easily graspable—as are prototypical props.[11]

What an ecological approach affords the performance analyst, then, is a relative ease in recognizing that a singular object onstage may equally afford manipulation, sitting on, masking, costuming, or even puppetry. While Bruce McConachie, in his brief discussion of the term, is surely correct that directors consider affordances "every time they block a scene," there is clearly more to affordances than blocking. Importantly, that they afford the above kinds of functional classifications does not equate affordances with either functions or stable categories. In the neat formulation of cognitive philosopher Mark Johnson, "objects" as such may actually be but "stable affordances" for us—most of them so stable, though, that they appear "to have fixed essences and to be observer-independent givens." In less ontological terms, Sofer does have a point in restricting the concept of props to situations of physical manipulation, but as for the audience—and for much of the actors' work—it need not matter much what you call them: "To perceive an affordance is not to classify an object," as Gibson makes some effort to emphasize. Subscribing to Wittgenstein's ideas of family resemblance, for classes of things, he insists "[y]ou do not need to classify and label things to perceive what they afford." What this comes down to, basically, is that not all objects we perceive as sit-on-able need be designed as such: we may well sit not only on chairs but on beds and tables, as well as on natural ledges or prop ledges or indeed on prop chairs actually designed to collapse on us. Understood as a *field of potential affordances* for the actors to engage in, the material reality of the stage stands out as both *enabling* and *constraining* their performances—"for good or ill," as Gibson had it, affordances can also take on a "negative" valence and downright resist our intentions (as in the case of what Sofer dubbed the "recalcitrant" prop).[12]

On Design and Pretense: Intentional, Immediate, and Improvised Affordances

So, affordances are not the same as functions, nor are they unidirectional "causal" influences, irrespective of ecological reciprocity. Search the term on the Internet, however, and most of what you get will relate to industrial design and computer interfaces (just think of the affordances of desktops and trash bins). As these design issues are crucial for the construction and use of theatrical props, as well, let us give them due consideration. In a nutshell, while Gibson himself already noted that "things can lie," authors like Donald Norman have since recognized the job of the designer in making the affordances visible—if you don't know how to open a door, it's not you who's to blame but poor design. In the theatre, however, not only can props be designed to behave differently than the "real thing" allegedly would—consider again the prop chairs' "hidden" affordance of collapsing—but, in principle, you can use any prop differently from its designed "proper" functions. While the latter have been dubbed the *intentional, conventional,* or *canonical* affordances of designed artifacts, these remain separate from such "first-order" affordances as have variously been called *immediate, physical, sensorimotor,* or even *natural*—in the sense that your regular mailbox does afford inserting litter, for instance, if you happen (or choose) to remain oblivious of its socially agreed uses.[13] In the theatre, we might add "performed" or "improvised" affordances to this range of what is physically possible, the point being that these can always override the range of what is considered "proper" to the context—which brings us to another interesting analogy.

In what has been written on affordances and *pretend play,* one proposition is that children first perceive the "intentional" affordances of objects (say, that socks are for wearing) and then come to detach or decouple these to engage in imaginative play—using socks as pretend guns, say. In more straightforward terms, however, "pretend objects need to support pretend acts, not real acts," as developmental psychologist Ágnes Szokolszky notes. "[A] pretend knife does not need to afford cutting, it only needs to afford *pretend cutting* which is a much less definite act" (comparable, of course, to the action force of Veltruský's prop dagger). On the one hand, then, the child only needs to select an object that is good enough to support her playful intentions—on the other, the enactment remains constrained by the properties of the object, as well: socks may afford "being used as pretend guns, but do not make good pretend houses, nor even swords," as Alan Costall and Ole Dreier elaborate. In the theatre, the looseness of this "pretense constraint" can surely be related to the genre of the performance as well as to its pursued level of realism, but on a more general level, it may be the only thing that really sets playful uses of objects apart from such unconventional uses as we engage in every day. As a detached object, for instance, a book may well afford not only reading but propping open a window or another book, as well as sitting—for an infant, given it's thick enough—and even food, if only a termite can digest it. Given its physical properties, the book will not afford just anything, but these are all real, practical uses—completely "proper" to the task at hand, while violating only its socially constructed proper function of "readability."[14]

Finally, pretend play is seldom an altogether solitary activity, and most certainly it is not in the context of a theatrical performance. Consider, again, the simple act of an actor sitting down, and how this may afford a lighting cue, for instance, for the light board operator. On the most general level, therefore, what is being implied here is a host of other *agents* apart from the stage actors (who may indeed do well in only engaging the basic-level affordances that are of most immediate concern for their performances). For the playwright, for instance—and here I will be brutally paraphrasing Sofer's ideas—simple props can afford not only "establishing character" or "animating stage action" (let alone "padding" the narrative or "tying up [its] loose ends"), but also "anchoring" or "energizing" whole scenes or indeed plays, as well as "confronting dramatic convention," "revitalizing theatrical practice," and "subverting conventional symbolism." Concomitantly, his "production analysis" approach implies the potential affordances of dramatic *texts* ("the horizon of [their] performance possibilities") for performance and scholarship—"find[ing] new affordances in the text that enable us to use it to do new work," as Bill Worthen has phrased it. Along similar lines, when Bert States reads the theatrical *chair* as "territorial preserve, weapon and shield (Ibsen and Pinter)" or as "the seat of anxiety . . . (Chekhov and Beckett)," we can take this as his list of its phenomenal affordances. In short, what we arrive at is an altogether different "order" of theatrical affordances, beyond but merging with those that are immediate or intentional, as for the objects onstage, or improvised by actors on the fly.[15]

Affordances for Interpretation

To sum up, then: If the "field of potential affordances" on the stage both enables and constrains what the actors can actually perform therein, then over time their performances will again enable and constrain what the spectators can possibly *make of it*—affording certain interpretations and excluding some others. Again, anything will not afford just anything: an "ecologically valid" performance analysis has to be based on what there is to be perceived (on what the stage invites, as it were), with an acute eye on the baseline materiality of theatrical objects, say, discussed by Rokem—but note the ontological stakes this kind of ecological epistemology implies. While admitting that humans have altered the very face of the earth (to change what it affords them, basically) and have done so in radical and often disastrous ways, Gibson would ultimately deny even the traditional distinction between "nature" and "culture" as misleading. For Gibson, there was "only one world," laid out in substances and surfaces whether these be natural or modified. A related dichotomy he wished to unpack was that between "material" and "non-material" culture, implying as it seems that "language, tradition, art, music, law, and religion are immaterial, insubstantial, or intangible, whereas tools, shelters, clothing, vehicles, and books are not": from a perceptual point of view, as he quite convincingly argues, "[n]o symbol exists except as it is realized in sound, projected light, mechanical contact, or the like." In Willmar Sauter's terminology, we need to recognize that all "artistic" or "symbolic" levels of theatrical interpretation have to be perceptually specified as the event unfolds; as Sauter himself attests, "nothing is symbolic unless perceived as such by the observer."[16]

From an ecological point of view, this perceptual grounding of interpretation—no matter how cultural or ideological in orientation—is generally agreed on by all more or less Gibsonian accounts of different art forms I know of, most notably in the musical hermeneutics of Eric Clarke. In short, he finds the most abstract and social of musical values to be "directly specified in the sounds themselves to a suitably attuned perceiver," whether she conceives of what she hears as "over-the-top singing" or as "Verdi's Rigoletto." Given how affordances always have to do with action—in his rather extended sense that music affords dancing or foot-tapping or marching or waiting on the telephone or taking drugs or playing air guitar—Clarke importantly acknowledges that "interpretation is also action: the speaking, writing, gesturing, and grimacing in which interpretation is manifest." To cite his example, "the recapitulation of the first movement of Beethoven's Ninth Symphony affords writing (or speaking) about in terms of murderous sexual rage, or the heavens on fire," but not in terms of "world-weary indifference" since the latter has "semantic requirements which this material cannot meet."[17] (A bit tongue in cheek, going back to States's discussion of theatrical chairs, we might then suggest that a traditional performance of Chekhov will not afford an interpretation of the characters actually standing up for themselves.)

As for how theatrical props may come to afford interpretations, more generally, we might do well in isolating Clarke's phrase—"in terms of"—and relating it to how we often make sense of abstract phenomena *metaphorically,* that is, in terms of more literal, "easy-to-grasp" experiences—especially those of perception, movement, and manipulation, central as they are for the sorts of ecologies we inhabit, in the playhouse and out. In such cognitive terms as furthered by Lakoff, Johnson, and others, "metaphor" would not be "figure of speech," as much as a ubiquitous way of thinking and acting—movement and manipulation, grounding our very concepts of *causation,* for example. The most abstract, social, and metaphysical varieties included, the prototypical case comes down to *object manipulation,* by a "human agency acting via direct physical force," which, of course, is pretty much what theatrical props instantly afford. As Gibson suggested in the 1960s (as if anticipating the theory of conceptual metaphor) there is "an element of perception in the appreciation of even the most abstract law"—and Lakoff and Johnson's own examples are full of implicit references to what their proposed "source domains" afford, for good or ill: "if ideas are objects, we can *dress them up in fancy clothes, juggle them, line them up nice and neat*"; metaphorical "difficulties" come as blockages, burdens, features of the terrain (as in: *He got over his divorce; Get off my back; It's been uphill all the way*). On the one hand, then, "the limits of the affordances of my world are the limits of my imagination," as Chris Sinha wittily paraphrases Wittgenstein; the way we perceive actors perceiving, interacting, moving about, and handling objects, delimits the range of how we come to understand the performance (especially if we don't share their language). On the other hand, again, we cannot really "design" audience response in advance, taking shape as it does within the ecological reciprocities of the whole theatrical event.[18]

Having elaborated Gibsonian approaches to spectatorship elsewhere, the larger implications on which I would like to end this overview essay lay, however, in the ecological grounding I argue these processes ultimately rely upon. In early Prague School terms, what we need to recognize is the primacy of action value—indeed equated with theatricality, by Veltruský and his colleagues—for perception and interpretation. Understanding "action" in terms of affordances, and "meaning" in terms of action, what we round up with is Veltruský's fundamental thesis that "one of the most important social objectives of the theater" lies in its "question[ing] the relationship between man and things with respect to activity." In the concluding section, I will try to show how this formulation anticipates important recent approaches to action, agency, and cognition. While the *metaphorical* sense we make of dramatic "causation," say, will likely keep working with well-worn scripts of subjects acting on objects (or occasionally, vice versa), the ecologies we actually engage in—onstage or off—imply more complex processes of reciprocal or mutual influence, causally continuous and cumulative, rather than mechanistic or unidirectional. Once we loosen our anthropocentric views of agents and artifacts, and allow for a fuzzier boundary, again, between *ourselves* and our environments, we begin to see the fundamentally distributed character of agency and cognition, which, I shall propose, is implicit already in Veltruský's early extensions of semiotic subjectivity. Finally, if "subjects" and "objects" are "really just abstractions from the interactive flow of organism-environment transactions," as Johnson argues, stage objects no longer appear "at the bottom of [a metaphorically vertical] hierarchy of theatrical elements" (as Sofer summarized the traditional "subject-oriented" position), but in horizontal networks of metonymical implication and ecological reciprocity.[19]

Action Force All the Way Down?

To begin to untangle these admittedly demanding concepts, consider Carl Knappett's bracingly clear-cut formulation: "Agency is not something we confer on objects in a one-way relationship [but] emerges reciprocally as humans and nonhumans merge." Terminology aside, this division of labor is reminiscent not only of Veltruský's—between what he calls the "basic subject" and the "partial subject," or, "the originator of the intent" and the one "overtly performing the action"—but of the "primary," intentional agents and the "secondary" artifactual agents anthropologist Alfred Gell would discuss some half a century later. Thought of as agents *barring intentionality,* stage objects need not turn into full-blooded subjects "equivalent to the figure of the actor," as per Veltruský, yet neither (and Andrew Sofer might disagree) are they only agents "in a manner of speaking," should we go with Gell's line of thought. Convincing in its simplicity, his argument is that for any agent and patient to interact, there has to be physical mediation of some kind: allowing for its *distribution* in what he terms "the causal milieu," it is only the secondary agents that render primary agency effective, "objectification in artefact-form," the only way for social agency to have impact. Or consider sociologist Bruno Latour's discussion of whether people or guns kill people: refusing the dualistic, "asymmetrical" terms of standard materialist and sociological explanations (that *either* guns or people do), he denies that either alone is the "actor," apart from the "hybrid" they form in conjunction. Again, there is no causation without coupling—the threat of the gunman, as that of Veltruský's dagger, is a compound affordance of the weapon and its wielder. As recent theorists of "material agency" suggest, rather than "debating what or who is or is not an agent," we should consider agency "as a situated process in which material culture is entangled."[20]

And what better example to flesh this out than the one theatrical prop we've occasionally used as a seat of discussion, all along. As many will remember, Bert States regarded the inauguration of the *chair,* on the realistic stage of the 1850s, as a great "preconventional shock" that affected the whole phenomenology of its acting. For the first time, a simple prop came to articulate the characters' relations to their social milieu, bodily binding the actors, as well, to the concrete stage world here and now. Come Bertolt Brecht, and we find him discussing his famous notion of the *gestus* in terms of the chairs and tables provided for him by his "stage-builder" Caspar Neher: as their relative height could make those sitting at the table bend over in "a quite specific attitude," if the two did not create attitudes, their legs were simply shortened until they did. To paraphrase McAuley, these props afforded not only specific gestures to enact, but whole "lifestyles" to represent onstage—and indeed a like range of affordances would accompany the introduction and use of chairs, outside of the theatre. According to historian Charles Fitzgerald, quoted by Rokem in his essay on the subject, there is "no aspect of furnishing and decoration which is not profoundly modified by the use of the chair when it replaces the mat": apart from their "need [of] tables raised high enough to fit the legs underneath," chair-sitters "will also sleep on raised beds." In effect, a similar argument can also be found from Marshall McLuhan, writing of chairs as an "extension of our backsides" that inevitably alters what he calls the "syntax of society"—in this case, creating the need for tables and other specifically measured furniture, quite in line with Fitzgerald's history, above. (And note, with anthropologist Tim Ingold, that "[t]he 'sitting society' to which we are so accustomed today is largely a phenomenon of the last 200 years.")[21]

In Gibsonian terms, what this comes down to is his understanding of an animal's ecological *niche*—beyond the false dichotomy of culture and nature—as a set of affordances: as opposed to *habitat,* the term refers "more to *how* an animal lives than to *where* it lives," the two being complementary in that "[t]he niche implies a kind of animal, and the animal implies a kind of niche." (Note also the theatrical metaphors often applied to the term: conventionally, a *niche* is defined as the "role" of the animal in its environment, even in an "ecological theatre" of "evolutionary play"; on a theatrical stage, concomitantly, what I've been calling the field of its potential affordances also delimits the possible roles/niches the actors/characters may come to "inhabit.") In Veltruský's terms, again, these examples relate to his discussion of action force as a function of "scenic metonymy." Important for our understanding of stage props, under any definition—ranging from their regular "shorthand" functions, for locale or identity, to what Sofer dubs their "fetishized" and "haunted" uses—I would propose defining the notion of metonymy in more cognitive terms, again, as a conceptual stand-for relationship in which one entity *affords access* to another. Importantly for the present discussion, this relationship works reciprocally in both directions: not only can an object stand for an action (Veltruský's "action force," motivating also the materialist interpretation of Latour's gun example), but mere action may equally evoke an absent object (as in Veltruský's discussion of "invisible props"). On both accounts—the ecological and the metonymical—agents and objects stand out as interdependent, interimplied, and interdefined; prior to metaphor, as Veltruský suggests, the "precise dramatic meaning" of theatrical objects "derives from acting by means of metonymy."[22]

Finally, what applies to props and objects, applies reciprocally to actors and characters. "Mutually complementary" with stage action, again by metonymy, the *stage figure* is for Veltruský a "dynamic unity" not only of "the actor's body, voice, movements, but also [of] various objects, from parts of the costume to the set." In his later work, especially, he suggests this figure "comprises not only a dramatic character in the naive sense," but "images" of the performer and the spectator, as well as "of the same character as projected by related stage figures and actions." Thoroughly implicated in metonymical networks of parts and wholes, "not only does every actor contribute to the creation of several stage figures but . . . every character . . . is represented by the work of several actors." From a characterological point of view, this emphasis on the "metonymic potential" of acting as a primarily *collective* enterprise also resonates with Bert States's account of how "every character trait" (compare the necessary and sufficient *properties* we didn't find in stage properties) can only unfold as an actual "event in the plot." "[M]ade of Gertrude and Claudius" and all the others, Hamlet is for States but a "collection of relationships" and, as such, not really "portable and adaptable" to other relationships. And where States argues that "[r]emoving a character from a play is like trying to pull up an oak tree," cognitive philosopher Alva Noë adds that every one of us is "like the plant itself," not like a mere berry to be plucked—*in and of* our soil, to the extent that when "transplanted" from our props, we ourselves are altered or even "disfigured." Reminiscent as this may be of naturalistic or expressionistic stagecraft—in the sense of States's "theatrical rooms" memorably "inhabit[ing] the people who inhabit them," the "causal masquerading as the casual"—Noë insists that this "isn't poetry," but "a well-supported empirical hypothesis."[23]

To conclude with a humble proposal on what the next stage of cognitively oriented theatre research might want to look like, the ecological direction, then, is firmly "out of our heads," as Noë proclaims. As James J. Gibson and Gregory Bateson knew already, the mental world "is not limited by the skin" (compare Pavis's difficulties in delimiting the actor from her surroundings). While the current framework of "embodied cognition" does deny the ontological distinction of *mind* and *body,* what it does not imply is that the Mind be the Brain—a metaphor that has indeed tempted many (McConachie, for instance, frames even affordances in terms of "mental images"). As philosopher Andy Clark puts it, the biological brain as such is cognitively "incomplete"; what he objects to, more specifically, is reducing all the rest of our cognitive ecology to mere "scene setting," under "the illusion that the mechanisms of mind and self can ultimately unfold only on some privileged stage marked out by the good old-fashioned skin-bag." What he endorses, again in resolutely theatrical language, is the crucial role of "nonbiological props" in the whole cognitive ensemble, "not just [as] aids for understanding the mind, but as key parts of the minds we seek to understand." Once we abstain from regarding our cognitive props as but accidental extras to a biologically given mind, we begin to move from what could be dubbed a *theatricality* of cognition (world as scene setting) to frameworks that begin to betray its fundamental *performativity*—from metaphors of internal mind, to ones of organism-environment coupling, and to how "meaning" is performed or "enacted" therein. On the one hand, then, it is not only brains or neurons that afford thinking; on the other, the "shifting coalition" of props and tools that does—neural and nonneural—may not even need a "privileged user," in the end. For Clark, we are "just tools all the way down."[24] Perhaps, if we wish to rescue them from the "bottom" of our field's hierarchies of interest, we should think of theatrical props along similar, ecologically informed lines.

Notes

1. Patrice Pavis, *Dictionary of the Theatre: Terms, Concepts, and Analysis* (Toronto: University of Toronto Press, 1996), s.v. "object"; Patrice Pavis, *Analyzing Performance: Theater, Dance, and Film* (Ann Arbor: University of Michigan Press, 2003), 15–16; Manfred Pfister, *The Theory and Analysis of Drama* (Cambridge, UK Cambridge University Press, 1991), 271–72; Jiří Veltruský, "Man and Object in the Theater," in *A Prague School Reader on Esthetics, Literary Structure, and Style,* ed. and trans. Paul L. Garvin (Washington, DC: Georgetown University Press, 1964), 87–88. The epigraph is from Andrew Sofer, *The Stage Life of Props* (Ann Arbor: University of Michigan Press, 2003), v.

2. Veltruský, "Man and Object," 87–88; Sofer, *Stage Life of Props,* vi, 9–10, 12, 29; Gay McAuley, *Space in Performance: Making Meaning in the Theatre* (Ann Arbor: University of Michigan Press, 1999), 179–80. McAuley cites Marcel Jousse from his *L'Anthropologie du geste* (Paris: Gallimard, 1974), 61.

3. Primarily associated with the early work of Eleanor Rosch and her associates, the most extensive introduction to cognitive categorization to date remains George Lakoff, *Women, Fire, and Dangerous Things: What Categories Reveal about the Mind* (Chicago: University of Chicago Press, 1987). See also George Lakoff and Mark Johnson, *Philosophy in the Flesh: The Embodied Mind and Its Challenge to Western Thought* (New York: Basic Books, 1999), 27–28; and Eve Sweetser, "Categories, Genres and Labels, Oh My . . . Thoughts on Art and Categorization from a Cognitive Linguist" (http://www.interstitialarts.org/why/categories_genres_1.html, 2003, accessed August 17, 2009).

4. Lakoff, *Women, Fire, and Dangerous Things,* 51. The prototypical notion of ecology is quoted from Kevin de Laplante, "Toward a More Expansive Conception of Ecological Science," *Biology and Philosophy* 19 (2004): 263.

5. For representative accounts of the field, see Bruce McConachie and F. Elizabeth Hart, eds., *Performance and Cognition: Theatre Studies and the Cognitive Turn* (London: Routledge, 2006); Bruce McConachie, *Engaging Audiences: A Cognitive Approach to Spectating in the Theatre* (New York: Palgrave Macmillan, 2008); and the December 2007 special issue of *Theatre Journal* (59, no. 4). For a recent discussion of the ecologies of "embodied cognition," see Mark Johnson, *The Meaning of the Body: Aesthetics of Human Understanding* (Chicago: University of Chicago Press, 2007).

6. For film and music, see Joseph D. Anderson, *The Reality of Illusion: An Ecological Approach to Cognitive Film Theory* (Carbondale: Southern Illinois University Press, 1996), and Eric F. Clarke, *Ways of Listening: An Ecological Approach to the Perception of Musical Meaning* (Oxford: Oxford University Press, 2005). For the earlier "nods" at Gibson or affordances, in theatre studies, see W. B. Worthen, *Drama: Between Poetry and Performance* (Chicester: Wiley-Blackwell, 2010); McConachie, *Engaging Audiences,* 73–74; Phillip B. Zarrilli, "An Enactive Approach to Understanding Acting," *Theatre Journal* 59, no. 4 (December 2007): 635–47; Zarrilli, *Psychophysical Acting: An Intercultural Approach after Stanislavski* (London: Routledge, 2009); Howard Mancing, "See the Play, Read the Book," in *Performance and Cognition,* ed. McConachie and Hart, 189–206; and Rush Rehm, *The Play of Space: Spatial Transformation in Greek Tragedy* (Princeton, NJ: Princeton University Press, 2002). For more generally "ecological" considerations of performance, see Baz Kershaw, *Theatre Ecology: Environments and Performance Events* (Cambridge: Cambridge University Press, 2007).

7. James J. Gibson, *The Ecological Approach to Visual Perception* (Hillsdale, NJ: Lawrence Erlbaum, 1986/1979), 127; emphasis in original. Emerging as relative to Jiří Veltruský and Marcel Jousse, in the present discussion, see also Gibson's own remarks tracing the lineage of his concept to Gestalt psychologists Kurt Koffka and Kurt Lewin. Gibson, *Ecological Approach,* 138–40. Curiously, Baz Kershaw refers his own use of "affordances" to a dictionary definition of the verb "to afford," with no mention of Gibson whatsoever. Kershaw, *Theatre Ecology,* 18. That the noun has also found its way to present editions of the *OED* bespeaks the steadily growing influence of Gibson's concept. *Oxford English Dictionary,* http://www.oed.com (accessed August 17, 2009). The heading of this section owes to Gregory Bateson, *Steps to an Ecology of Mind* (Chicago: University of Chicago Press, 1972).

8. Gibson, *Ecological Approach,* 127–28, 140–41, and passim. See also James J. Gibson, *Reasons for Realism: Selected Essays of James J. Gibson,* ed. Edward Reed and Rebecca Jones (Hillsdale, NJ: Lawrence Erlbaum, 1982), 405; and *The Purple Perils: A Selection of James J. Gibson's Unpublished Essays on the Psychology of Perception,* http://www.trincoll.edu/depts/ecopsyc/perils (accessed August 17, 2009).

9. Gibson, *Ecological Approach,* 16–18, 128; Gibson, *Reasons for Realism,* 407–8, emphasis in original.

10. Gibson, *Reasons for Realism,* 411; Gibson, *Ecological Approach,* 126, 128; Harry Heft, "Affordances and the Body: An Intentional Analysis of Gibson's Ecological Approach to Visual Perception," *Journal for the Theory of Social Behaviour* 19, no. 1 (1989): 1–30, esp. 10, 18–19. See also Eleanor J. Gibson and Anne D. Pick, *An Ecological Approach to Perceptual Learning and Development* (Oxford: Oxford University Press, 2000), and Harry Heft, "Affordances, Dynamic Experience, and the Challenge of Reification," *Ecological Psychology* 15, no. 2 (2003): 149–80, esp. 173–76. For the affordances of theatrical training, see Zarrilli, "Enactive Approach" (e.g., page 646: "The actor engaged in certain forms of training builds a repertoire of sensorimotor skills that afford various possibilities of action within the theatrical environment").

11. Sofer, *Stage Life of Props,* 12; Veltruský, "Man and Object," 87; McAuley, *Space in Performance,* 176; Freddie Rokem, "A chair is a Chair is a CHAIR: The Object as Sign in the Theatrical Performance," in *The Prague School and Its Legacy,* ed. Yishai Tobin (Amsterdam: John Benjamins, 1988), 276–88, esp. 278; Harry Heft, "Affordances of Children's Environments: A Functional Approach to Environmental Description," *Children's Environments Quarterly* 5, no. 3 (1988): 29–37; Gibson, *Ecological Approach,* 34, 39, 133, 307. In general outline, the latter distinction is in agreement with Erika Fischer-Lichte's semiotic understanding that the performance space and its decorations "allow for" *proxemic* signs, whereas the concept of "props" is more connected with the actors' intentional *gesture*—however, the latter remain "difficult to categorize" for the semiotician, as props "can also function as elements of other . . . sign systems." Fischer-Lichte, *The Semiotics of Theater,* trans. Jeremy Gaines and Doris L. Jones (Bloomington: Indiana University Press, 1992), 107. To an extent, the sort of creativity that goes into extending prototypical conceptions of categories can be seen as a function of affordances, on a basic level of action and cognition: insofar as they are distinguished by affording manipulation, stage props need not even be inanimate, as Andrew Sofer argues in his present contribution.

12. McConachie, *Engaging Audiences,* 74; Johnson, *Meaning of the Body* 47; Gibson, *Ecological Approach,* 127, 134, 137; Sofer, *Stage Life of Props,* 24.

13. Gibson, *Ecological Approach,* 138–39, 143; Donald A. Norman, *The Psychology of Everyday Things* (New York: Basic Books, 1988); Michael Tomasello, "The Cultural Ecology of Young Children's Interactions with Objects and Artifacts," in *Ecological Approaches to Cognition: Essays in Honor of Ulric Neisser,* ed. Eugene Winograd, Robyn Fivush, and William Hirst (Mahwah, NJ: Lawrence Erlbaum, 1999), 153–70; Harry Heft, *Ecological Psychology in Context: James Gibson, Roger Barker, and the Legacy of William James's Radical Empiricism* (Mahwah, NJ: Lawrence Erlbaum, 2001), 345. See also Heft, "Affordances and the Body," 17–18; Alan Costall, "Socializing Affordances," *Theory and Psychology* 5 (1995): 467–81, esp. 471–72; and Carl Knappett, *Thinking through Material Culture: An Interdisciplinary Perspective* (Philadelphia: University of Pennsylvania Press, 2005), 47–50, 58. Notably, central as it is to his discussion of drama, Worthen only refers his use of affordances to Norman, who appropriated the term from Gibson. Worthen, *Drama,* 21–22.

14. Tomasello, "Cultural Ecology," 154, 157–60, 166; Alan Costall and Ole Dreier, eds., *Doing Things with Things: The Design and Use of Everyday Objects* (Aldershot, UK: Ashgate, 2006), esp. Introduction, 4; and Ágnes Szokolszky, "Object Use in Pretend Play: Symbolic or Functional?" esp. 68 and 81–83. See also Clarke, *Ways of Listening,* 37–38.

15. Sofer, *Stage Life of Props,* vii, x, xii, 3–5, 13, 22; Worthen, *Drama,* 34; Bert O. States, *Great Reckonings in Little Rooms: On the Phenomenology of Theater* (Berkeley: University of California Press, 1985), 46.

16. Rokem, "A chair is a Chair is a CHAIR," 285; Gibson, *Ecological Approach,* 129–30; and James J. Gibson, *The Senses Considered as Perceptual Systems* (Boston: Houghton Mifflin, 1966), 26; Willmar Sauter, *The Theatrical Event: Dynamics of Performance and Perception* (Iowa City: University of Iowa Press,

2000), 6–8. In psychology, "ecological validity" refers to experiments conducted outside the artificial conditions of laboratories.

17. Clarke, *Ways of Listening,* 38, 45–46, 204; see also States, *Great Reckonings,* 73–74.

18. Lakoff and Johnson, *Philosophy in the Flesh,* esp. 177–78, and George Lakoff and Mark Johnson, *Metaphors We Live By* (Chicago: University of Chicago Press, 1980), 13, emphasis in original; Gibson, *Senses Considered as Perceptual Systems,* 286; Chris Sinha, "Blending out of the Background: Play, Props and Staging in the Material World," *Journal of Pragmatics* 37, no. 10 (2005): 1542n4. For a good overview of conceptual metaphor theory, see Zoltán Kövecses, *Metaphor: A Practical Introduction* (Oxford: Oxford University Press, 2002); for further references on its use in theatre studies—and there is a small tradition, already—see McConachie and Hart, eds., *Performance and Cognition.*

19. Veltruský, "Man and Object," 83, 91; Jiří Veltruský, "Puppetry and Acting," *Semiotica* 47, no. 1 (1983): 87; Johnson, *Meaning of the Body,* 67; Sofer, *Stage Life of Props,* v. On reciprocal causality, see Heft, "Affordances and the Body," 6, 10. On the fuzzy boundaries of agency, see Knappett, *Thinking through Material Culture,* 11–12, 15–16, 22–23, 29–30, 62, 85; and Carl Knappett and Lambros Malafouris, "Material and Nonhuman Agency: An Introduction," in *Material Agency: Towards a Non-Anthropocentric Approach,* ed. Knappett and Malafouris (New York: Springer, 2008), esp. ix–xiii. For a Gibsonian account of theatrical spectating, see my "On Spectatorship, Objecthood, and the Enaction of Visual Experience" (in the 3rd Yearbook of the Theatre Research Society in Finland, Laura Gröndahl, Teemu Paavolainen, and Anna Thuring, eds., 2009, available at http://www.teats.fi/TeaTS3.pdf).

20. Knappett, *Thinking through Material Culture,* 28; Veltruský, "Man and Object," 83, 88; Alfred Gell, *Art and Agency: An Anthropological Theory* (Oxford: Clarendon, 1998), 20–22. Bruno Latour, *Pandora's Hope: Essays on the Reality of Science Studies* (Cambridge, MA: Harvard University Press, 1999), 176ff., is discussed in Knappett, *Thinking through Material Culture,* 30–31, and in Knappett and Malafouris, "Material and Nonhuman Agency," xi–xii, whence also the citation at the end of the paragraph.

21. States, *Great Reckonings,* 42–43; John Willett, ed. and trans., *Brecht on Theatre: The Development of an Aesthetic* (New York: Hill and Wang, 1992), 231; McAuley, *Space in Performance,* 180–82, 202; Rokem, "A chair is a Chair is a CHAIR," 275; Marshall McLuhan, *Understanding Media: The Extensions of Man* (Corte Madera, CA: Gingko Press, 2003), 7, 250; Tim Ingold, "Culture on the Ground: The World Perceived through the Feet," *Journal of Material Culture* 9, no. 3 (2004), 323. Ingold's humble thesis is that "the boot and the chair establish a technological foundation for the separation of thought from action and of mind from body" (ibid.). Rokem quotes Fitzgerald from his *Barbarian Beds: The Origin of the Chair in China* (Canberra: Australian National University, 1965), 3–4.

22. Gibson, *Ecological Approach,* 128–30, emphasis in original; Veltruský, "Man and Object," 88; Sofer, *Stage Life of Props,* 20–21, 26–27; Veltruský, "Puppetry and Acting," 85, 87. On metonymy, see Kövecses, *Metaphor,* 143–62. *The Ecological*

Theatre and Evolutionary Play is the title of a monograph by G. E. Hutchinson (New Haven: Yale University Press, 1965).

23. Veltruský, "Man and Object," 84; Veltruský, "Puppetry and Acting," 70, 104–5, 112–13; States, *Great Reckonings,* 46, 67, 143, 148–49; Alva Noë, *Out of Our Heads: Why You Are Not Your Brain, and Other Lessons from the Biology of Consciousness* (New York: Hill and Wang, 2009), 65, 69. Especially when it comes to his discussion of mere traveling as a mild form of being "transplanted," Noë's point was well brought home to me, reading his book, as I did, during my trip to the Theatre Symposium.

24. Noë, *Out of Our Heads;* Gibson, *Ecological Approach,* 41; Bateson, *Steps to an Ecology of Mind,* 339, 460; McConachie, *Engaging Audiences,* 73; Andy Clark, *Natural-Born Cyborgs: Minds, Technologies, and the Future of Human Intelligence* (Oxford: Oxford University Press, 2003), 4–6, 27, 136–37, 189–90, 192; Andy Clark, "Author's Response," *Metascience* 13 (2004), 169, 180. On embodied cognition, see Johnson, *Meaning of the Body;* on cognitive ecology, look for Edwin Hutchins's essay so titled, forthcoming in *Topics in Cognitive Science.*

"Take up the Bodies"

Shakespeare's Body Parts, Babies, and Corpses

Andrew Sofer

THE *OXFORD ENGLISH DICTIONARY* defines a stage property as "[a]ny portable article, as an article of costume or furniture, used in acting a play; a stage requisite, appurtenance, or accessory."[1] As I argued in *The Stage Life of Props,* a prop can be more rigorously defined as "a discrete, material, inanimate object that is visibly manipulated by an actor in the course of performance."[2] Irrespective of its signifying function, a prop is something an object becomes, rather than something an object is: an object must be "triggered" in some way by an actor (like Osric's hat in *Hamlet*) in order to be a prop. But if any *thing* can become a prop, does this necessarily mean that *any*thing can become a prop? What of the human body itself?

From the perspective of semiotics, "All that is on the stage is a sign."[3] According to the principle of semiotization (which Umberto Eco calls ostension), a cup on the stage automatically becomes the sign "cup."[4] But if so, it becomes virtually impossible to decide what *isn't* an object onstage, including the actor. Indeed, for Martin Esslin, the actor's body is the "iconic sign *par excellence:* a real human being who has become a sign for a human being."[5] In his landmark 1940 article "Man and Object in the Theater," Prague School structuralist Jiří Veltruský acknowledges the difficulty of separating subject from object onstage and instead posits a fluid continuum between them. In Keir Elam's gloss of Veltruský's argument, objects are "promoted" up the scale "when they are raised from their 'transparent' functional roles to a position of unexpected prominence" and acquire "semiotic subjectivity" independent of the actor.[6] To use Veltruský's own example, a stage dagger might move from being a passive emblem of the wearer's status to participating in the action as an instrument of murder, and thence to a final independent association with the concept "murder." Conversely, when the actor's "action force" is reduced to zero, the actor takes on the status of a prop (for example, a spear carrier or corpse). From this semiotized point of view, actor and prop are dynamic sign-vehicles that move up and down the subject-object continuum as they acquire and shed action force in the course of a given performance. For Veltruský, an object becomes a prop when it begins to take part in the action overtly as a tool; and when props acquire independent signifying force, "we perceive them as spontaneous subjects, equivalent to the figure of the actor."[7]

Veltruský's concept of the subject-object continuum invites us to think more flexibly about under what circumstances human bodies—or parts of bodies—might become props. When I first considered whether the human body could become a prop, or whether props were by definition inanimate, I concurred with Gay McAuley, who in *Space in Performance* writes: "For some analysts the body of the actor is an object, indeed the primary object on stage. . . . but I would say that, although a part of the body, or even a whole body, can become an object if so treated (touched, carried) by another actor, it is unhelpful to assimilate the inanimate and animate, to place into the same category subject and object. The scandal of treating a person or animal as object is muted if all bodies are routinely classified as objects."[8] I commented: "If subjects can be objects on stage, then everything counts as an object, and the category of 'object' becomes meaningless."[9] This essay represents a rethinking of my own position. For if theatrically mobilized objects such as Yorick can take on a life of their own, cannot immobilized subjects become dead objects—taking on, as it were, a *death* of their own in performance?

Motionless bodies crop up with some regularity onstage, fascinating us in their oscillation between dead character and counterfeiting actor. Early modern tragedies tend to end with a frozen tableau of dead bodies, which we are invited to enjoy—if that is the word—as a three-dimensional *tableau mort.* Having explored the ventriloquized skull on the Jacobean stage, an object posing as a subject, it seems a logical next step to turn attention to the stage corpse, a subject posing as an object.[10] And where better to look than to Shakespeare, surely the ideal laboratory for any investigation into how dramatists exploit theatre's phenomenological possibilities? Moreover, the stage corpse highlights the very scandal to which the fungibility of bodies and objects draws our attention: the possibility that actors' bodies are mere objects or tools of the dramatist, director, or even spectator. "Do not talk of him / But as a property," sneers Antony, instrumentalizing Lepidus as a tool in *Julius Caesar* (4.1.39–40).[11]

Under what circumstances, then, can the human body become a prop? Certainly body *parts* can and do become props. We need only think of the skulls that populate dramas such as *Hamlet* and *The Revenger's Tragedy*. Stage skulls are not bodies, properly speaking, except as (dead) metonyms. The same goes for severed heads, which make notable appearances in *Titus Andronicus* and *Macbeth*.[12] Cloten's head and headless body make separate appearances in *Cymbeline;* both are used as props. Such body parts challenge the playwright, prop maker, and actor. Severed limbs and bodies threaten to break the dramatic illusion, since they are patently fake. Moreover, there is the problem of how to handle and remove them—especially if the character has no arms, as in the case of the one-armed Titus and his mutilated daughter, Lavinia, who have one hand between them at the point in the play where Titus is confronted with the grotesque sight of the heads of his two sons, Quintus and Martius. "Come brother, take a head," Titus instructs Marcus, "And in this hand the other will I bear; / And, Lavinia, thou shalt be employ'd; / Bear thou my hand, sweet wench, between thy teeth" (3.2.279–82). It is hard to see how tragedy avoids farce here. But perhaps that is the point, since the tonally unstable *Titus* is in part(s) about the propensity of tragedy to collapse into grand guignol. The play walks the tightrope between pathos and bathos, tragedy and sick humor—as when Tamora, barbarous Queen of the Goths, swallows her just desserts in the form of a pie baked out of her two sons. The scandal of treating body parts as props underscores Russell Fraser's wise dictum that "the rude handling of sacred totems is what the drama is all about."[13]

If severed limbs are clearly props—the pilot's thumb in *Macbeth,* the wax hand in *The Duchess of Malfi,* the severed finger in *The Changeling*—what of babies? It would be hard to argue that babies do not also function as hand-props, but their theatrical use presents further difficulties. Live babies threaten the dramatic illusion through their unpredictability. They may distract attention from the scene through wailing, wriggling, and so forth; they may disrupt tone and genre, gurgling happily when the fictional baby is supposed to cry, or vice versa, moving the audience to amused laughter. If real babies are more trouble than they are worth—"Never work with animals or children," W. C. Fields reputedly warned—then the use of fake babies runs its own risks. It is almost impossible to build a convincingly "live" prop-baby, although director Peter Brook notes that an audience will magically accept a non-iconic substitute baby in the hands of a skilled actor.[14]

Perhaps this explains why Elizabethan and Jacobean drama calls for relatively few infants. Aaron the Moor's bastard child appears in several scenes in *Titus Andronicus.* The stage direction "*Enter Nurse with a blackamoor child*" suggests that a doll may have been used (4.2.51ff.). The action involving this prop-baby is tricky. Aaron must take his baby from the nurse with one hand, while threatening the young Goths Chiron and Demetrius and stabbing the nurse with the other—all without dropping the cuddled baby. No actor would risk dropping (or stabbing) a real child. It is therefore up to the actors to "animate" the doll prop, which presumably is wrapped in some sort of blanket, as is suggested by Aaron's query to the nurse, "What dost thou wrap and fumble in thy arms?" (4.1.58). Aaron puts Chiron and Demetrius in charge of dragging off the nurse's body, leaving him free to carry the baby off stage as a prop: "Come on, you thick-lipp'd slave, I'll bear you hence" (4.2.175).

In the play's final scene, following the slaughter of Titus and his enemies, the baby is uplifted to the view as a badge of Tamora's shame. "Behold the child," Titus's brother Marcus solemnly intones from the upper stage (5.3.119). If the child is held aloft by Marcus, rather than by an attendant—the text is unclear on this point—Marcus may here turn his back to the groundlings and raise the child toward the noble "Roman" spectators in the upper gallery of the playhouse. If so, Marcus's quasi-blasphemous echo of John 19:5 in the Vulgate translation ("*ecce homo*") suggests that the actor mimics the gesture of a priest at Mass.

After this early *coup de théâtre,* Shakespeare for the most part avoids onstage babies, perhaps having concluded after his *Titus* experience that they are more trouble than they are worth. Another notable Shakespearean infant (or infanta) is the future Queen Elizabeth I, who appears as a prop held by an actor at the climax of the collaborative play *Henry VIII,* a christening scene in which Archbishop Cranmer delivers an encomium to the future Virgin Queen (and Shakespeare's prior monarch). Here the baby-as-prop is not only "ostended" in Eco's sense, but fetishized as a sacred icon: "*Enter trumpets, sounding; then two Aldermen, Lord Mayor, Garter, Cranmer, Duke of Norfolk with his marshal's staff, Duke of Suffolk, two Noblemen bearing great standing-bowls for the christening gifts; then four Noblemen bearing a canopy, under which the Duchess of Norfolk, godmother, bearing the child richly habited in a mantle, etc., train borne by a lady*" (5.5. s.d.). Archbishop Cranmer's blessing of Elizabeth goes on for some fifty lines, the scene itself for seventy-six—plus a procession about the stage. Elizabeth remains the focus of the scene; at one point King Henry kisses her. Would Shakespeare's company have dared use a live baby as its central prop?[15] It seems unlikely, but it is hard to say for sure. In an era in which at least one playhouse doubled as a bearbaiting pit, the well-being of someone's baby may not have been uppermost in the players' minds. At least the nascent actor, if incorporated as a touch of realism, had no lines to forget.[16]

As the cultural valence of staged corpses has been discussed elsewhere, the remainder of this essay will focus on the practical and dramaturgical issues raised by bodies as props.[17] When an actor dies onstage, he is playing an object and must conform to the very definition of a prop offered by the *OED*. But an actor playing a dead body is not merely a nonce-thing. The stage corpse, hovering in our imagination between subject and object through a kind of cognitive dissonance, may paradoxically accrue more Veltruský́an action force than a live character. Homer Swander usefully reminds us that "[a] corpse on stage demands attention."[18] For the actor, *dying* is not the problem. As Tom Stoppard's down-at-heels Elizabethan player boasts, "It's what the actors do best. They have to exploit whatever talent is given to them, and their talent is dying. They can die heroically, comically, ironically, slowly, suddenly, disgustingly, charmingly, or from a great height."[19] The challenge is not playing dead, but *staying* dead. Put another way, the ambitious corpse must upstage the living without being too obvious about it. Concealment of the breath is not that hard to accomplish, especially with the careful placement of the arms over the abdomen, but if one chooses to die with one's eyes open, not blinking becomes a challenge. To quote Michael Green's invaluable *The Art of Coarse Acting:* "If a fight ends in death be sure to die in a comfortable position. Once again ignore any director who wants an actor to hang around for half a scene draped over a grandfather clock or some such nonsense. My advice to the aspiring body is to die behind something and then have a good sleep. If one is in view there is always the danger of heavy breathing or even a sneeze, apart from the strain of having to lie still."[20]

The Elizabethan corpse's greatest hurdle was neither playing nor staying dead, but getting himself off stage as a moveable. No curtain hung across the Elizabethan stage, and plays were performed in daylight, so there could be no blackout between scenes. The decorous disposition of corpses is an especial problem in tragedy (we might call it the Polonius problem). Crudely put, there are few dignified ways to remove a stage corpse. While some playwrights of the time seem to have left the problem of how to get bodies off stage to the actors, Shakespeare as expert theatre practitioner characteristically finds or invents several ingenious dramaturgical solutions to a pressing theatrical problem.

The playwright's simplest course is to have the character die off stage à la Ophelia or Lady Macbeth. But ultimately, there must be (visible) blood, and the Elizabethan audience, weaned off the Senecan convention of offstage carnage by the lurid revenge tragedies of Kyd and others, would no doubt have felt cheated not to witness the death of its tragic hero (scattered limbs, as in the B-text of *Doctor Faustus,* were no doubt a bonus). Thus the stage direction following Macduff's killing of Macbeth reads, "*Enter fighting, and Macbeth slain*" (5.8.34 s.d.). Since theatre is not cinema, and the camera cannot simply cut to the next frame, the Macduff actor must carry off Macbeth's body before reappearing with the head prop.

A second solution is to draw a discreet curtain around the dead. At the climax of *Othello,* the Moor stabs himself and conveniently falls on the bed in the "discovery space" where the strangled Desdemona and her maid Emilia already lie thanks to Emilia's forethought ("Ay, ay! O, lay me by my mistress' side" [5.2.237]). "Look on the tragic loading of this bed," commands Lodovico. "The object poisons sight, / Let it be hid" (5.2.363–65). Lodovico's verbal stage direction suggests that the bed's canopy, or possibly the discovery-space curtain, is simply drawn around the bed-property—itself a thrust stage within a stage—concealing the "object" from sight.

Shakespeare's third option is to make corpses responsible for their own removal by having them jump into the stage trap. As Mariko Ichikawa points out, this seems to work best in cases where characters take their own lives (for example by jumping into a river), but is also adaptable to stage murders. *Macbeth*'s stage directions do not specify how Banquo's assassins remove his corpse. Ichikawa conjectures that, given the later reference to him being "safe in a ditch," the murderers may have cast Banquo's body into the stage pit (3.4.25). The Banquo actor could then have used the trap for his entrances and exits in the banquet scene.[21]

A fourth recourse is just to cart the bodies off. This seems to be the default method in Elizabethan and Jacobean drama, if only because it was preferable to having corpses make their own exits. Were stagehands involved (themselves, perhaps, the prop's prop)? According to Ichikawa, "there is no evidence [from surviving manuscript playbooks] that stage attendants performed the task of carrying corpses offstage."[22] Rather, in cases when leading actors did not do so, supernumeraries would have performed the task "in character" as soldiers or servants. And yet the expedient solution is hardly the most elegant. The unwieldiness of a supine actor, especially a portly one, invites mirth, especially if the actors are trying to maintain tragic decorum.

Hence Shakespeare tends to make a virtue of necessity and to thematize the very indignity of the process of turning a person into a prop—precisely the scandal noted by McAuley. Thus Hamlet's former superciliousness toward Polonius translates into his rough handling of the ministerial remains at the close of the "closet" scene:

> This man shall set me packing;
> I'll lug the guts into the neighbor room.
> Mother, good night indeed. This counselor
> Is now most still, most secret, and most grave,
> Who was in life a foolish prating knave.
> Come, sir, to draw toward an end with you.
> Good night, mother. (3.1.211–17)

As stage direction, the First, "Bad" Quarto edition (Q1, 1603) gives "*Exit Hamlet with the dead body*"; the Second Quarto (Q2, 1604–5) just "*Exit*"; the First Folio (F, 1623) has "*Exit Hamlet tugging in Polonius.*" At this point Richard Burbage presumably slipped his hands under the Polonius-actor's armpits and dragged him upstage through one of the tiring house doors. Shakespeare underscores the mordant comedy of theatrical corpse removal, turning what should be a grave undertaking into something almost Pythonesque:

> KING: Now Hamlet, where's Polonius?
> HAMLET: At supper.
> KING: At supper? Where?
> HAMLET: Not where he eats, but where 'a is eaten; a certain convocation of politic worms are e'en at him. Your worm is your only emperor for diet; we fat all creatures else to fat us, and we fat ourselves for maggots; your fat king and your lean beggar is but one variable service, two dishes, but to one table—that's the end. (4.3.16–24)

Yet the prince's vicious Eucharistic satire, nailed down by the ghastly pun on the Diet of Worms, is more than mere mockery. *Hamlet* addresses a key anxiety in (supposedly) Protestant England regarding where people go when they die. It is impossible to tell whether Ophelia's death is a suicide; we do not know the fate of Hamlet's soul. Every death in the play is hugger-mugger, every funeral a "maimed rite." *Hamlet* arguably ends not with the cathartic ennoblement of tragedy, but with a messy heap of dead bodies. Interestingly, a play that begins with the visitation of a corpse come to life ends with another talking corpse: "I am dead, Horatio" (5.2.333). Hamlet speaks his last speech uncannily both dead and alive.

How is the final scene to be cleared of its tragic loading? Shakespeare craftily places a verbal stage direction in the mouth of Fortinbras, who with a splendid lack of imagination (he has not seen the play) decrees that Hamlet shall have the soldier's funeral he himself would desire:

> Let four captains
> Bear Hamlet like a soldier to the stage,

For he was likely, had he been put on,
To have prov'd most royal; and for his passage,
The soldiers' music and the rite of war
Speak loudly for him.
Take up the bodies. Such a sight as this
Becomes the field, but here shows much amiss.
Go bid the soldiers shoot. (5.2.395–403)

As Ichikawa notes, it is uncertain whether Shakespeare's intent here is to clear the stage of actors.[23] Q2 has Fortinbras command "Take up the bodies," signaling that Claudius, Gertrude, and Laertes are to be treated as props. But Q1 and F's line "Take up the body" implies that only Hamlet is to be carried as a prop, and that Laertes, Gertrude, and Claudius remain as stage furniture until the play ends. It remains unclear what the line "Bear Hamlet like a soldier to the stage" indicates, given that Hamlet is already *on* stage. Perhaps Hamlet is to be carried to a raised platform (possibly the one on which the duel transpired) or to the upper stage as a fetishized sign, achieving full semiotic subjectivity as an inanimate prop.

Death's ignoble properties compound in the case of another late Shakespearean corpse, Antony in *Antony and Cleopatra*. Antony's demise is among the most protracted in Shakespeare. Having heard (falsely) that Cleopatra is dead, Antony bids his companion Eros slay him. Eros kills himself instead, leaving Shakespeare an extra stage body to deal with. More an antique Roman than a Dane, Antony falls on his own sword but botches the job: "How, not dead? not dead? / The guard, ho! O, dispatch me!" (4.14.103–4). Three guards enter but refuse to finish Antony off, although they graciously round out his anguished lines into more decorous blank verse. Another companion, Diomedes, enters, and Antony, whose stage position is ambiguous ("Art thou there, Diomed?"), issues an anguished plea: "Draw thy sword, and give me / Sufficing strokes for death" (4.14.116–17). Having imparted the news that Cleopatra is not dead after all but locked in her monument, Diomedes calls the guard once more. Antony issues another verbal stage direction: "Take me up. / I have led you oft; carry me now, good friends, / And have my thanks for all" (4.14.138–40). The guards bear Antony (and presumably Eros) off as a prop. Again, Shakespeare undermines tragic *gravitas* by emphasizing the clumsiness of the action.

In the following scene, Cleopatra and her female entourage appear "*aloft*" on the upper stage at the back of the main stage, which now signifies the monument. The guard and Diomedes enter on the main stage below, bearing the injured Antony (possibly in some kind of fireman's lift). At this point, the 1623 Folio text (the earliest text, whose precise but impractical stage directions suggest it derives from Shakespeare's foul papers rather than from a promptbook) becomes uncertain. Cleopatra twice indicates her desire to draw Antony aloft, and Antony repeats, "I am dying, Egypt, dying" (5.15.18, 41). This may indicate Shakespeare's uncertainty about how to handle the situation (Cleopatra's first "Help, friends below, let's draw him thither" at 5.15.13 may be an uncanceled false start). A strange moment ensues where the men below hoist Antony aloft to the women above. Once more, Shakespeare thematizes the recalcitrant weight of human bodies, along with the sheer manual labor attendant on his art:

> CLEO: Help me, my women—we must draw thee up.
> Assist, good friends.
> ANOTONY: O, quick, or I am gone.
> CLEO: Here's sport indeed! How heavy weighs my lord!
> Our strength is all gone into heaviness,
> That makes the weight. Had I great Juno's power,
> The strong-wing'd Mercury should fetch thee up,
> And set thee by Jove's side. Yet come a little—
> Wishers were ever fools—O, come, come, come.
> *They heave Antony aloft to Cleopatra.*[24]
> And welcome, welcome! Die when thou hast liv'd,
> Quicken with kissing. Had my lips that power,
> Thus would I wear them out. (5.15.30–39)

After a final lovers' exchange, Antony dies, and Cleopatra faints. Once she awakens, Cleopatra orders her attendants to bury Antony, and the scene's final stage direction reads "*Exeunt, bearing off Antony's body*" (5.15.91 s.d.). Embodying the slide down the subject-object continuum in excruciating slow motion, Antony is by turns lively and deadly prop.

The fourth method of corpse removal is to bring the dead to their feet. Obviously, however, the corpse could not simply rise (or even crawl) and exit without ruining or, more charitably, alienating the effect. The notion of a stage corpse springing to life at the end of a scene or play jolts us. Ichikawa concludes that early modern stage corpses only came to life at the very end of plays (whose epilogues occasionally call for applause to raise the dead). While embracing such non-illusionistic strategies as the aside and the soliloquy, early modern drama evidently steered clear of sending corpses scrambling for cover at the end of the scene. Thus in fighting scenes, victors must have been responsible for carrying off their dead. Ichikawa cautions: "If an onstage corpse should walk off, the role/actor balance would break down and the imaginary world would be shattered: the corpse should therefore be either borne out as if to another fictional place that is supposed to exist behind the stage or it should simply be hidden in order to prevent it becoming a visual distraction."[25]

For Maria Doyle, the spectacle of a reanimated body subversively ruptures catharsis. "[T]he traditional pleasure of tragedy comes not just from the expulsion of emotions but also from the dispersal of feelings that might be deemed dangerous or messy; the audience needs the death/demise of the hero to cleanse itself. [Playwright Marina] Carr's denial of catharsis is, thus, a denial of this cleanliness, of the audience's impulse to pass over the explanations and intellectual argument presented in the middle of a play because of the intense emotional release that finality brings."[26] But there is no evidence Shakespeare read Aristotle's *Poetics,* let alone the Greek tragedians, so perhaps we moderns have un-Elizabethan attitudes to tragic decorum. Elizabethan and Jacobean audiences were used to genre friction. Plays such as *Doctor Faustus* lurch between high tragedy and knockabout comedy, and as Thomas Dekker testifies in his *Strange Horse-Race* (1613), "I have often seene, after the finishing of some worthy Tragedy, or Catastrophe in the open Theaters, that the Sceane after the Epilogue hath beene more blacke (about a nasty bawdy Jigge) than the most horrid Sceane in the Play was."[27]

Shakespeare exploits the jarring metatheatricality of what we might call the "zombie" solution to corpse removal for comedic ends at the close of *1 Henry IV.* Two fights occur simultaneously at the Battle of Shrewsbury. On one side of the stage, glamorous Prince Hal fights his rival, Hotspur; on the other, Douglas the fearsome Scot fights the crapulent Falstaff. Falstaff and Hotspur both fall, and the audience presumes them both dead. When Hal reenters and serially eulogizes the corpses, the bodies accrue action force. Indeed, they strikingly juxtapose the two *genres* Hal must choose between: history on the one hand and comedy on the other. Throughout the play, Hotspur has embodied the principle of honor through martial valor, whereas Falstaff has married a refusal to take anything seriously to a cynical philosophy in which honor is but a "word" (5.1.134). For much of the play, Hal has been happy to frequent comedic space, as represented by the Eastcheap tavern; but he must now forsake tavern for court and take up the mantle of history as England's future King Henry V.

Hal's eulogy for Hotspur is delivered in high rhetorical mode, as Hal honors his fallen rival by covering his mangled face with his royal "favors" (plumes). Then Hal notices the corpse of his fat, dissolute friend and delivers a mock eulogy over the motionless figure:

What, old acquaintance! Could not all this flesh
Keep in a little life? Poor Jack, farewell!
I could have better spar'd a better man.
O, I should have a heavy miss of thee
If I were much in love with vanity!
Death hath not strook so fat a deer to-day,
Though many dearer, in this bloody fray.
Embowell'd will I see thee by and by,
Till then in blood by noble Percy lie. (5.4.102–110)

Having delivered his mock-heroic eulogy, the prince exits the stage, and we seem to be left alone with a (tragic?) corpse. Much to our delight, Falstaff springs up like a jack-in-the-box to address us in prose soliloquy while "nobody" is looking:

> Embowell'd! if thou embowel me to-day, I'll give you leave to powder me and eat me too tomorrow. 'Sblood, 'twas time to counterfeit, or that hot termagent Scot had paid me scot and lot too. Counterfeit? I lie, I am no counterfeit. To die is to be a counterfeit, for he is but the counterfeit of a man who hath not the life of a man; but to counterfeit dying, when a man thereby liveth, is to be no counterfeit, but the true and perfect image of life indeed. The better part of valor is discretion, in the which better part I have sav'd my life. 'Zounds, I am afraid of this gunpowder Percy though he be dead. How if he should counterfeit too and rise? By my faith, I am afraid he would prove the better counterfeit. Therefore I'll make him sure, yea, and I'll swear I kill'd him. Why may he not rise as well as I? Nothing confutes me but eyes, and nobody sees me. Therefore, sirrah [*stabbing him*], with a new wound in your thigh, come you along with me. (5.4.111–28)

In a delightful variant on the fourth solution, "*He takes up Hotspur on his back*" (5.4.129). Falstaff then encounters Hal and his brother, John, dropping Hotspur at their feet. Hal bids Falstaff take up the body once again: "Come bring your luggage nobly on your back" (5.4.156). Shakespeare ingeniously solves the problem of removing Hotspur's property-corpse, which has no place in the play's final scene, while deftly managing an allusion to the Devil carrying off Worldly Man in William Wager's morality play *Enough Is as Good as a Feast* (1560). In a crowning thematic irony, Hotspur, "the theme of honor's tongue" (1.1.81), is literally objectified as comedic "luggage"—an unusually inconvenient prop.

Human limbs, skulls, babies, and corpses each stretch my original definition of properties as "a discrete, material, inanimate object." As final evidence, I cite a possibly apocryphal story recounted by the eighteenth-century antiquarian William Oldys (as reported by George Steevens in

1793). According to Oldys, once King Charles II reopened the playhouses in 1660 following the Restoration, a group of actors questioned one of Shakespeare's younger brothers (now in old age) regarding Shakespeare's acting:

> The actors were greedily inquisitive into every little circumstance, more especially in Shakespeare's dramatic character, which his brother could relate of him. But he, it seems, was so stricken in years, and possibly his memory so weakened by infirmities, that he could give them but little light into their inquiries; and all that could be recollected from him of his brother Will in that station was the faint, general, and almost lost ideas he had of having once seen him act a part in one of his own comedies, wherein being present to personate a decrepit old man, he wore a long beard, and appeared so weak and drooping and unable to walk, that he was forced to be supported and carried by another person to a table, at which he was seated among some company who were eating, and one of them sang a song.[28]

This description clearly matches the feeble retainer Adam, carried in on the shoulders of Orlando in *As You Like It*. For the bard's own brother, apparently, Shakespeare's most memorable performance was as a prop.

Notes

1. *The Compact Edition of the Oxford English Dictionary* (Oxford: Oxford University Press, 1971), s.v. "property."
2. Andrew Sofer, *The Stage Life of Props* (Ann Arbor: University of Michigan Press, 2003), 11.
3. Jiří Veltruský, "Man and Object in the Theater," in *A Prague School Reader on Esthetics, Literary Structure, and Style,* ed. and trans. Paul L. Garvin (Washington, DC: Georgetown University Press, 1964), 84.
4. Umberto Eco, "Semiotics of Theatrical Performance," *Drama Review* 21 (1977): 107–117.
5. Martin Esslin, *The Field of Drama: How the Signs of Drama Create Meaning on Stage and Screen* (London: Methuen, 1987), 56. For a feminist counterargument that "placing the 'dead' [female] body at the structural center of the drama" leads "the observer beyond the icon of the body into a more complex appreciation" of character, see Maria Doyle, "Dead Center: Tragedy and the Reanimated Body in Marina Carr's *The Mai* and *Portia Coughlan,*" *Modern Drama* 49 (2006): 41–69.
6. Keir Elam, *The Semiotics of Theatre and Drama* (London: Routledge, 1980), 17.
7. Veltruský, "Man and Object," 84.
8. Gay McAuley, *Space in Performance: Making Meaning in the Theatre* (Ann Arbor: University of Michigan Press, 1999), 176.

9. Sofer, *Stage Life of Props,* 211.

10. Ibid., 89–115.

11. All citations from Shakespeare's plays are from *The Riverside Shakespeare,* 2nd ed., ed. G. Blakemore Evans et al. (Boston: Houghton Mifflin, 1997).

12. Shakespeare probably wrote *Titus Andronicus,* his earliest tragedy, with George Peele. See Brian Vickers, *Shakespeare, Co-Author: A Historical Study of Five Collaborative Plays* (Oxford: Oxford University Press, 2002), 148–243.

13. Russell A. Fraser, introduction to *Drama of the English Renaissance I: The Tudor Period,* ed. Russell A. Fraser and Norman Rabkin (New York: Macmillan, 1976), 3. Fraser's principle perhaps reaches its ultimate extreme in the cannibalistic drama of Sarah Kane, raising the question of whether the rude handling of sacred objects is *all* the drama is about.

14. Peter Brook, *There Are No Secrets: Thoughts on Acting and Theatre* (London: Methuen, 1993), 46.

15. If played by a boy, "Elizabeth" would have been a cross-dressed role; if played by a girl, perhaps the first instance of a female appearing on the professional English stage.

16. At *Henry VIII*'s first recorded performance, on June 29, 1613, cannon fire accidentally set fire to the Globe Theatre's thatched roof. The show literally brought the house down.

17. For the cultural signification of stage corpses, see Pascale Aebischer, *Shakespeare's Violated Bodies: Stage and Screen Performance* (Cambridge, UK: Cambridge University Press, 2004); and Valerie Traub, "Jewels, Statues, and Corpses: Containment of Female Erotic Power," in *Desire and Anxiety: Circulations of Sexuality in Shakespearean Drama* (London: Routledge, 1992), 25–49. On Shakespeare's handling of stage corpses, I am indebted to Mariko Ichikawa, "What to Do with a Corpse?: Physical Reality and the Fictional World in the Shakespearean Theatre," *Theatre Research International* 29 (2004): 201–15; and to Homer Swander, "No Exit for a Dead Body: What to Do with a Scripted Corpse?" *Journal of Dramatic Theory and Criticism* 5 (1991): 139–52.

18. Swander, "No Exit," 139.

19. Tom Stoppard, *Rosencrantz and Guildenstern Are Dead* (London: Faber and Faber, 1967), 61.

20. Michael Green, *The Art of Coarse Acting* (New York: Limelight, 1987), 53.

21. Ichikawa, "What to Do with a Corpse?" 208–9.

22. Ibid., 203.

23. Ibid., 212.

24. Here Shakespeare may conceivably be debasing the notion of deaths on the upper gallery as nobler than deaths on the main stage. The convention of cross-dressing complicates the scene's "gendered" division between upper, "female" stage and lower, "male" stage. For the possible design and use of Cleopatra's monument, see Andrew Gurr and Mariko Ichikawa, *Staging in Shakespeare's Theatres* (Oxford: Oxford University Press, 2000), 63–64.

25. Ichikawa, "What to Do with a Corpse?" 212–13.

26. Doyle, "Dead Center," 49. In the Boston Actors' Shakespeare Project

2009 production of Webster's *The Duchess of Malfi*, Jennie Israel (as the duchess) simply rose to her feet and walked off stage after being strangled.

27. Quoted in Andrew Gurr, *The Shakespearean Stage 1574–1642*, 3rd ed. (Cambridge, UK: Cambridge University Press, 1992), 175.

28. Quoted in *As You Like It: A New Variorum Edition*, ed. Horace Howard Furness (Philadelphia: J. B. Lippincott, 1890), 130–31.

Contributors

Kyna Hamill is a lecturer in the Core Curriculum program at Boston University. She is currently doing research on weaponry and visual culture in the seventeenth century. She has a forthcoming article in *Print Quarterly* and a chapter in *Performance of Violence in Contemporary Ireland*. She edited *They Fight: Classical to Contemporary Stage Fight Scenes* (2003), a collection of theatrical combat scenes. She is a member of the Popular Entertainment working group for International Federation for Theatre Research (IFTR) and serves as a contributing editor to *Popular Entertainment Studies*.

Andrew Kimbrough received his MFA in acting from Carnegie Mellon University and the Moscow Art Theatre School, and his PhD in theatre from Louisiana State University. He is an assistant professor of theatre at the University of Kentucky.

Adrienne C. Macki is an assistant professor in dramatic arts at the University of Connecticut. Her work has been published in *Theatre Journal*, *New England Theatre Journal*, *Journal of American Drama and Theatre*, *Theatre History Studies*, and the *Encyclopedia of Ethnic American Literature*. She has received fellowships from the American Association of University Women, the American Society for Theatre Research, and the Driskell Center for the Study of the Visual Arts and Culture of African Americans at the University of Maryland.

Christopher J. Mitchell is an associate professor of theatre arts at Eastern Illinois University and is an affiliated faculty member of the Women's Studies and Film Studies programs. Dr. Mitchell's areas of scholarly interest include the plays of August Strindberg, feminist theatre, Scandinavian theatre and film, and European realism/naturalism of the late nineteenth and early twentieth centuries. He is also an active dramaturg and director.

Stefani Overman-Tsai is a graduate student at California State University, Stanislaus. She received her BA in theatre arts and communications from Whittier College and her MA in theatre arts from California State University, Sacramento. She has also taken graduate-level classes at Louisiana State University.

Eleanor Owicki is a PhD student in the Performance as Public Practice program at the University of Texas at Austin. Her primary interest is in Irish theatre, and she received an MA from the University of Texas with a thesis entitled "Our Day Will Come? Female and Catholic Identities in Northern Irish Theatre" in the spring of 2008. Her dissertation will explore performances of memory and identity in Belfast after the 1998 Good Friday Agreement.

Teemu Paavolainen expects to finish his PhD dissertation on performer-object interaction in Grotowski, Kantor, and Meyerhold in 2010 (that will be in English). In Finnish, he has published on puppetry and cognition, Jerzy Grotowski, Tadeusz Kantor, and Samuel Beckett. Theatrical objects and Polish performances aside, his theoretical expertise resides in recent "ecological" approaches to action, perception, and cognition, variously dubbed embodied, enactive, extended, situated, or distributed.

Sarah Powers is a doctoral candidate in theatre arts at Cornell University, where she focuses on ancient Greek and Roman theatre, spectatorship, and farce. She earned her BA in classics and theater studies from Emory University and has also worked as the literary intern at the McCarter Theatre.

Andrew Sofer is associate professor of English at Boston College. His essays have appeared in *Theatre Journal, Modern Drama, Comparative Drama, Journal of Dramatic Theory and Criticism, English Literary Renaissance, The Oxford Handbook of Early Modern Theatre,* and *The Blackwell Companion to Twentieth-Century American Drama.* His book *The Stage Life of Props* (University of Michigan Press, 2003) received honorable mention for the 2004 Barnard Hewitt Award given by the American Society for Theatre Research. He is currently at work on a second book, *Dark Matter: Invisibility in Drama, Theatre, and Performance.*

Bland M. Wade Jr. is the director of the Stage Properties Program, School of Design and Production at the University of North Carolina School of the Arts. He has worked with many companies, including Heritage Repertory Theatre, Actors Theatre of Louisville, and the North Carolina Shakespeare Festival. He is a practicing artist with experiences in theatre, opera, dance, film, and television, as well as commercial and corporate events. He is a member of the International Alliance of Theatrical Stage Employees (IATSE) Local 635, the Society of Property Artisan Managers (S*P*A*M), the U.S. Institute for Theatre Technology (USITT), the Southeastern Theatre Conference (SETC), and the American Association of Woodturners (AAW).

Christine Woodworth is an assistant professor in the Department of Theatre at the University of North Carolina at Greensboro, where she teaches theatre history and serves as dramaturg. She holds a PhD from Bowling Green State University and an MA from Indiana University. Her articles and reviews have appeared in *Theatre Topics, Theatre Annual,* and *Text and Presentation.* She has also written a chapter for the collection *Theatrical Portrayals of Mothers: A Historical Tracking of Mothers, Mothering, and Motherhood through the History of World Theatre* (forthcoming from Edwin Mellen Press).